D0900931

JOY
UNSPEAKABLE

Toxic Faith
and Rose-Colored Glasses

JOY HOPPER

Copyright © 2017 Joy Hopper
All rights reserved
First Edition

PAGE PUBLISHING, INC.
New York, NY

First originally published by Page Publishing, Inc. 2017

ISBN 978-1-64082-445-4 (Paperback)
ISBN 978-1-64082-446-1 (Digital)

Printed in the United States of America

For Marni.

Thank you for decades of unconditional love and friendship, for politely enduring my shitty first draft, and for validating my memories with your own.

May we always keep our membership active in the mutual admiration club. I adore you and the raucous laughter you bring to my world. And I just want to say that "Br—— was a dick too."

Joy Unspeakable and Full of Glory
Barney Eliott Warren

I have found His grace is all complete,
He supplieth every need;
While I sit and learn at Jesus' feet,
I am free, yes, free indeed.

Refrain
It is joy unspeakable and full of glory,
Full of glory, full of glory;
It is joy unspeakable and full of glory,
Oh, the half has never yet been told.

Select Hymns, 1911 (Timeless Truths)

I was born with rose-colored glasses. Not literally of course. My real vision enhancements had clear lenses that were attached to my infant face with rubber bands. With my bald head and wire rims, I was affectionately nicknamed Tweety Bird. But more distinct than being a hairless, crossed-eyed wonder with spectacles was my uncanny ability, as I grew older, to see what others often missed—the cup half full, triumph in tragedy, humor in hardship, and empathy for the underdog—essentially, viewing the cosmos through a customized eyepiece designed specifically to distort reality. Some may regard this trait as altruistic—always looking for the good, even if it's the proverbial needle in the haystack. But for me, it was about finding meaning and making sense of the world. Sometimes seeing life in 20/20 is too painful for the human mind to process and it seeks to soften the edges and blur the lines as a way of making circumstances more palatable. This ability, whether innate or contrived, to look beyond the drama of the stage and imagine what was happening behind the curtain, enabled me to interpret, redefine, justify, and explain away every obstacle in my path.

It's from this mind-set that my fundamentalist Christian orientation became desirable from a very young age. My brain had a special way of sugarcoating the negative aspects of faith in Jesus so that the overarching theme was *joy*. The Bible proclaimed the *joy* of salvation, the *joy* of sins forgiven, the *joy* of eternal life, and the *joy* of being known and loved by the creator of the universe. In church, I sang about the "*joy, joy, joy, joy*, down in my heart" and proclaimed, "The *joy* of the Lord is my strength." This unspeakable *joy* was the driving force behind my virtuous ambitions—missionary, Sunday school teacher, church musician, songwriter, homeschool mom, home group leader's wife, women's ministry speaker, and above all, godly wife.

I was convinced that as a believer in Jesus, I had the corner on joy. Not only was it my name, it was also my identity. I was warned that without Christ, my life would be hollow and void of meaning and purpose, like the poor unfortunate, disillusioned atheists, gays, backsliders, sluts, gamblers, and other wretched sinners I had heard about in church, who would seek to fill that God-shaped void in all the wrong places. Joy, in this context, isn't solely about always being happy and bubbly; I think of it more as a by-product of believing that everything has a purpose and nothing happens by chance. It's being able to confidently navigate through life with a contented smile, even when circumstances look bleak, because there is an invisible force righting all wrongs and turning trials into triumphs.

This is my story of fundamental Christianity as viewed through my rose- colored glasses. Some affectionately refer to them as "God goggles" because when wearing them, invisible Jesus magically appears like a holograph, morphing each storyline into a Pollyanna object lesson. I'm eager to paint a vivid portrait of what my world looked like through the unique lens of faith. Every obstruction was an opportunity. Every disappointment was a refining tool. Unanswered prayers were examples of misguided desires. Virtually every circumstance, when viewed metaphorically, through my magic lenses, would draw me closer to my savior and bring meaning to life. When looking at others' misfortune, I could glibly respond, "But for the grace of God go I" and would proceed to thank God for sparing me the calamity that others couldn't escape. Yet upon closer examination, I'm now convinced the unspeakable joy that I claimed to possess was really more of a smoke screen to mask the unspeakable fear and dread my religion produced when the God goggles were removed. Without my rainbow filters, how could I even begin to fathom the indescribable horrors of hell, realizing that friends, loved ones and even myself could be consciously tortured for all eternity without even a halfway point in time served? Or how about the unrelenting evil power of the devil, who is constantly sneaking up on us, reading our minds and trying to harm, deceive, and even kill us? Or how can we sanely go about our business with the terrifying trauma of one day being snatched up into heaven in the rapture without even a second's warning, like a thief in the night, or worse, to be left behind to be brutally tortured and even beheaded by the Antichrist? Without my rose-colored glasses, how could I endorse and propagate a religion founded on human sacrifice and whose symbolic rituals include cannibalism—eating the flesh and drinking the blood of the slain victim? If Christianity was true, as I believed with all my heart it was, I needed my bright, enhanced overlay to claim and proclaim the unspeakable joy of knowing Jesus.

My purpose in sharing this story is to expose the unwritten, unseen horrors of fundamentalism when used to override natural instincts and interfere with rational decision-making. This seemingly benign and happy religion crippled me emotionally and psychologically with its fear tactics and continual toxic message that I was worthless, unlovable, and the object of God's wrath without Christ. I want to pull back the curtain to show what was happening behind the façade of my Christian bubble, not only in childhood and adolescence but also as an adult, with my God-ordained marriage, six adorable, obedient children, and the white picket fence. The external scaffolding creates a beautiful mirage of wholeness and health—a quality of life that others, especially in times of desperation, aspire to and the bait that often hooks the seeker, looking to religion for greener pastures. But behind the set lies the same brokenness familiar to all of humanity. For me, Christianity warped reality in such a way that I couldn't discern abuse from tough love, self-hatred from humility, human need from idolatry, or submission from misogyny. Consequently, I naively subjected myself to needless emotional trauma in the name of following Jesus.

Even more importantly, I am compelled to share the transformation that took place when my seemingly impenetrable beliefs became dismantled from my brick-and-mortar, steel-reinforced foundation and I saw my life for the first time without the distortion of my God goggles. A new me, I submit, the "real" me, emerged, full of confidence, purpose, joy, gratitude, and love, despite the pompous whispers circulating among the faithful about how tragic it was that

I was so "lost." I trust my story conveys loudly and proudly that I've never been more "found" and that by ridding myself of destructive, fundamentalist ideology, I have been given my life back.

My target audience is everyone—believers, unbelievers, once believers, wannabe believers. If you were brought up in the church, you will surely relate to the many Christian nuances woven into the tapestry of my experiences, especially if you were raised Pentecostal, *glory-da-god*. If you've never been a convert, you have a backstage pass to enjoy a sampling of what you may have missed while you were out being a normal human being. And if you too have discovered that your religious indoctrination no longer works for you, may you find comfort in my journey, knowing you are most certainly not alone.

A few names, places, and identifying details have been changed to maintain a cloak of anonymity, but otherwise, to the best of my ability, my memoir is true, warts and all.

Part One

Childhood
Immersion and Conversion

1

Fragments

Candy cigarettes.
Matt, Steve, Chris.
Old Daddy.
Jules.
Paper whistle tossed into the bathtub.
Screaming.
Tantrums.
Cowboy boots.
A bonk on the head with a door at a trailer park.
Matt peeling an orange for me, while I screamed in protest that he wasn't doing it right.

This was the sum total of my chapter 1, circa 1961–1965, pre-adoption. For twenty-three years, those pages were missing from my "book" as if they had been hastily ripped out, leaving sketchy remnants of words and sentences out of context and partial paragraphs and pictures with poor resolution.

Growing up, I tried to fill in the missing details with my own theories and assumptions about who I was and where I came from. Like a good detective, I used the clues left behind to recreate the setting, characters, and plot line, but I knew the account wouldn't be trustworthy until I found the original manuscript from which to compare my own rendering of events. So for my entire childhood and young adulthood, my story picked up at chapter 2, the day old Daddy got arrested for his second DUI.

2

Riding Pink Flamingos

My twin sister, Jules, and I were only three when the social worker showed up and whisked us away. We had been transported to a little farm on North Pleasant Valley Road, about forty miles from our home in Pocatello, Idaho. Our only earthly belongings accompanying us consisted of a small cardboard box of tattered clothing, matching yellow polka-dot rompers with elastic-gathered bloomers that we were wearing, and a small, blue plastic, double-sided rocking horse seat that still held a place in our hearts though we had long since outgrown it. When the social worker pulled up to the house, dust settling behind us from the gravel road, our new mama and daddy and grandmother, with her cooking apron and floral printed dress, greeted us in the yard. I remember eyeing the pink flamingo lawn ornaments propped up by wire legs beckoning my sister and I to come and ride. We exited the car and ran as quickly as our chubby little legs would carry us, right to the plastic birds, squealing, with toddler glee, "Horsies!" There was one for each of us, and with flawless synchronization, we jumped on our pink stallions as the wire legs buckled and sent us crashing to the ground. Our new mama smiled nervously and swept us up on our feet, making sure we were okay, hoping that our first impression wasn't a total disaster. Leaving the pink fowls lying on the grass with contorted legs, to be fixed later, she welcomed us inside the little red brick farmhouse, much like the one that withstood the huffing and puffing of the big bad wolf in the tale of *The Three Little Pigs*. The social worker said good-bye, kissing Jules and I on our cheeks and leaving crimson smudges from her bright-red lipstick, which made us giggle. And our new life in the Hoffmann family began.

While we were encouraged to call these strangers "Mama" and "Daddy," such terms were far too intimate even for displaced three-year-olds. So, at least initially, our preferred term of endearment, "Hey you," seemed to suffice. We didn't understand that this was our permanent home. We didn't know that we would never see our brothers or our "old daddy" again for the rest of our childhood. But the days turned into weeks and the weeks into months, and quite naturally, Roy and Jeannie became Daddy and Mama and the memories of our past family seemed to dissipate like the morning fog.

My mama was beside herself with joy to have twin daughters, and everyone who knew her would concur. She had married Daddy when she was sixteen to get away from her cruel and abusive stepmother, Marie. Before she had reached the ripe age of twenty, Mama had already given birth to three handsome boys. She wanted more kids, specifically some daughters, but had to let go of her dream after having an emergency hysterectomy at age thirty. But to her delight, her wish was granted five years later, when Jules and I landed on her flamingos and into her heart. The boys, Ray, Ron, and Steve, their biological children, who were much older, worked outside on the farm with Daddy, before and after school, moving pipe or driving tractor, which left the house empty most of the day, until we came along and became the focus of her motherly doting. And though she loved us dearly, she would often reminisce about the challenges she initially faced to train us. As she put it, we "could make sailors blush" by our expansive repertoire of vulgar expletives. The first time she heard "goddammit" and "what the hell!" spew from our little innocent mouths, she was taken aback. This was foreign and unwelcome jargon for a devoutly religious, fundamental Pentecostal Christian family in rural Idaho. She would immediately inform us sternly, "That's su'um we don't say!" And she would then briskly march us straight to the bathroom to wash the dirty, "devil" words off our lips. At first, we had no concept of words having discernable qualities and weren't even sure which ones were being scrubbed clean. But at some point, we started connecting the dots and identifying all bad words as "su'um we don't say." *Dumb, stupid, fool, idiot, shut up, pee-pee, darn, shoot,* and *heck* all made the list. Even *fart* was taboo, and so whenever we would let one slip, we would say, "Oops! I just did a su'um we don't say!" We honestly thought that was what *everyone* called it, until we were embarrassingly old enough to know better and mentioned it in *passing* (no pun intended) at school. That very well could've been the first faux pas that set us on our downward trajectory to social oblivion. Anyway, no matter how many times that soap-slathered toothbrush got shoved into our mouth, those naughty little demons continued to wrangle our tongues until eventually, our poor, abused taste buds raised their white flag in silent surrender.

We were also exceptional tantrum throwers who could very likely win a blue ribbon at the fair, if such a category existed for kicking, screaming, and holding one's breath. While Mama relied heavily on "traditional" discipline methods, such as spanking with Daddy's belt and shaming to train us, occasionally she would stray from her script and creatively invent a consequence to fit the crime. I remember one such incident, when I clinched my fists, curled the right corner of my upper lip, and started stomping my feet upon not getting my way. Mama immediately responded, "Oh, Joy! I see you like to march. Since you like it so much, you can just keep on marching." Confused and curious, I started marching in place, like a little soldier. At first it was kind of fun and I thought Mama was playing a game with me when she kept saying, "Get those knees up!" But after a minute or so, I lost interest and wanted to scamper off with my sister. But Mama said I wasn't done marching and that I needed to keep on going. After a while I realized Mama wasn't being silly. The spirited, sing-song, "Get those knees up, "started to sound more like a growling drill sergeant. "GET THOSE KNEES UP!" She had a scowl on her face that told me she meant business. So I kept on marching, up and down and up and down, in obligatory obedience. Each time I stopped, Mama said, "Keep going because I know you like to march!" Clearly this was a misunderstanding. I was not having even a tiny bit of fun. So I cautiously stuttered, "Mama, I . . . I . . . I don't like to march." She feigned surprise. "What?" she gasped. "You don't like to march? Are you sure? Then I don't ever want to see you stomping your feet again." Miraculously, it worked. Mama knew she was onto something, so she tried the same tactic to keep Jules and me from wildly swinging our legs from the pew, during church. "I see you like to swing your legs. Okay then, sit here and start swinging." And "Oh, I see you like to wet in your pants instead of going to the toilet. Why don't you just wear this baby diaper on the outside of your clothes?"

But even the most progressive discipline methods can backfire on occasion. One time, Jules and I got into the jellied candy stash, hidden in the top cupboard that Mama used to dip in white chocolate for Christmas goodies. When she discovered the bag half empty, or as I would prefer, "half full," Mama sat us down in the middle of the kitchen floor and scolded, "If you like these so much, you can just eat the whole bag! Go on now!" I'm not sure how well she had thought this one through. I mean, punishing kids with candy was akin to punishing Cheech and Chong with tainted brownies or Bill Clinton with young female interns and a box of cigars. But with the flair of true Shakespearian thespians, we pulled off a performance, Oscar-nomination worthy, by contorting our faces and holding our stomachs, all the while telepathically sharing our secret glee with nonverbal eyebrow twitches and quick winks. When she wasn't looking, we even fought over who would get to eat the last piece. After the bag was empty, we forced out a few belchy moans, as Mama smiled and nodded with smug satisfaction that once again, we had "learned our lesson."

3

The Holy Rollers

My fondest early childhood memories captured my twin and I donning matching dresses, with white-laced anklet socks and shiny patent-leather buckle shoes, our Sunday best, to attend the Pentecostal church in town. It was there that my sister and I were showered with kisses and subjected to affectionate cheek pinching. Joining the Hoffmann family was huge news in this little farming community, and we were celebrities of sorts—poor, wild little heathens with an alcoholic dad and no mama, "rescued," if you will, by a Christian family. We didn't just belong to Roy and Jeannie; we belonged to the entire church, and everyone made it their mission to take us under their wing and help discipline us in the ways of the Lord.

Sister Berquin invited us to her house once a week to "catch us up" on many of the children's songs that we would need to know in Sunday school. I'll never forget my favorites: "Climb, Climb Up Sunshine Mountain," "The B-I-B-L-E," "The Wise Man Built his House Upon a Rock," and of course, the venerated "Jesus Loves the Little Children." I can't say for sure, but I suspect the music lessons were initiated at the request of my Sunday school teacher, Sister Pauline. Let me just say, in my defense, how was I to know when she asked who had a favorite song, that the commercial jingle, "Winston tastes good, like a cigarette should," was *not* on the approved list?

In the main service, there was a plump old lady who always carried a tin canister with fruit-flavored lozenges in her purse, the kind that would sometimes stick together in the humidity, offering a celebratory two-for-one special when they couldn't be pried apart. It didn't take long for us to realize, in a true Pavlovian sense, if we either sat beside her or in the pew directly behind her, there was a very good chance we would be rewarded with one of her treats. The minute her purse clicked open, we were right there, salivating, as we eagerly awaited her invitation to partake. The joy between the giver and the receiver was mutual, as a happy bond was formed and sealed with little girl smiles and high-fructose corn syrup.

The church was our life on Sunday morning, Sunday evening, and family night on Wednesday. We were called Holy Rollers in the community because it was rumored that we would roll down the aisles and swing from the chandeliers. The perception didn't stray too far from reality. People shouted and danced in the aisles, speaking in tongues and prophesying. The messages transmitted directly from heaven to our congregation always started with, "Thus saith the Lord," and continued in King James English in honor of the creator of the universe's sixteenth-century official dialect. There were altar calls at each meeting where kids and grown-ups alike knelt to confess their sins or to get filled with the Holy Ghost. When congregants were sick, the pastor and the elders would lay hands on them, anoint their head with oil, and perform an exorcism of sorts, casting out the pesky demon of whatever ailed them. If I ever thought such behaviors were weird or bizarre, I don't recall. All I know is at some point, I accepted the whole package, and church became an integral part of my childhood, adolescence, and adulthood.

4

Adoption

When Jules and I were five, the adoption process was complete, and I distinctly remember Mama crossing out the name *Slater* that was inscribed in ink on a hardback story book we owned and replacing it with our new last name, *Hoffmann*. And though the courts had granted to us all the rights and privileges of natural-born children, our insecurities weren't easily absolved. The abrupt way in which we had been displaced from everything and everyone we knew left us anxious and fearful. The people to whom we had formed attachments from birth, Matt, Steve, Chris, and Old Daddy, were gone, and the emotional ties were irreparably severed without any process of closure. Social workers now understand that by helping children keep their existing attachments, they are better able to form healthy new ones. The questions started to flow as the reality began to sink in that we were at one time Joy and Julie Slater. Now we were Joy and Julie Hoffmann and we were never going back home. Why did we get sent away? How did we end up in the Hoffmann family? Did our old family love us? Would they remember us? Would we ever see them again? Would they want to see us? Were our brothers adopted too? Did they stay together? Mama would drop hints occasionally about the Slaters. but none of them were good. She said Old Daddy Dean was an alcoholic and didn't take care of us, and our mother, Lillie, had left when we were babies. Thus, our rendition of the missing pages of Chapter 1 began with, "We were neglected, abandoned, and unloved by our first parents." And whether our assumptions were true or not, the sting was very much real, leaving an ache that seemed to linger just under the radar of our fragile emotions. And if our "real" parents didn't want us, how could we trust the intentions of our new mama and daddy? For example, Mama used to jokingly threaten Ray, Ron, and Steve, saying, "If you boys don't behave, I'm gonna drop you off at the Reservation to live with the Indians!" Her sons knew it was in jest and would play along by dancing around with their hand on their mouth, pretending to be warriors doing a rain dance. But when we came along and she experimented on us, we burst into tears and promised to be good while begging her not to send us away amidst our anguished sobs. Mama felt as cheap as the faith healer snatching the invalid's crutches at the tent revival, only to watch him fall on his face when God didn't deliver. She realized as soon as the wailing erupted that perhaps threatening to abandon her newly adopted children for disobeying would not earn her the otherwise deserving Mother of the Year award. She tried to recant, but we never saw the Indian Reservation the same way after that. This was a learning process as much for the Hoffmanns as it was for us. Another time, we were in the hen house gathering eggs when we saw a diseased chicken with one huge bulging eye, like the Cyclops from Odysseus. "Looks like we need to chop her head off," Mama concluded, rather matter of fact, as if noticing the weathered fence needing paint or the creaking gate hinge begging for oil. Surprised and mildly horrified, I asked cautiously, "Why do you have to chop off her head?" Mama replied, "The chicken is sick, and so we have to kill her." The poor chicken with the huge bulging eye, vulnerable and oblivious to her doomed fate, was about to get the axe for being sick. My chest tightened and my eyes widened as I considered the ramifications. "Mama," I blurted, "If I get sick, are you going to chop my head off?" Mama's unabashed laughter assured me that the rules for chickens thankfully did not apply to children, but I certainly wasn't about to take any chances. This might partially explain why I could be burning up with fever or coughing up a lung and still insist on going to school. Fortunately, my high threshold for pain was rewarded with a "Perfect Attendance" certificate nearly every year of elementary school.

Everything I had ever known was challenged when joining the Hoffmanns. Mama would often say, "You may have been able to get away with that at the Slaters, but not in this family." That meant I needed to learn a whole new set of expectations—the terms and conditions of membership into my new clan. Everything I had assumed previously became obsolete, and I needed to understand and even test the boundaries of Mama and Daddy's love, which included "What happens if I get sick?" and "Will you still keep me if I misbehave?"

There were other clues as well, offering hints that I was still adjusting to emotional insecurities despite being welcomed in my new family. For one thing, I had recurring nightmares. One that plagued my sleep night after night for years took place in the chicken coop, the very place I had first encountered the bulging-eyed chicken slated for the chopping block. In my dream, however, the hen house became the witch's cottage from *Hansel and Gretel*, and Jules and I were the lost children. Every night, the witch who had lured us into her house with candy would capture Jules and me, and we would scream and fight with all our might to get away. Just as we were about to be thrown in the oven, I would wake up trembling, and as soon as I would close my eyes, the story would reset and the terror would continue. While I didn't understand the significance of my dream as a child, it's obvious to me now what my psyche was trying to work through. The idea of being "lost" with my sister bore a striking resemblance to being suddenly plucked out of our home, without warning and without closure, and taken out in the middle of nowhere on a farm in the country. The candy cottage mimicked the nice home we lived in that was inviting and even enticing when we first showed up, but once we stepped in, there was no going back. The threat of being thrown in the oven seemed to resonate the period of mistrust, wondering if the intentions of the Hoffmanns were good or bad and if they had our best interests at heart.

Mama would try to hold me on her lap and rock me to sleep, knowing that I had likely missed out on this type of nurturing without a mother in the picture. But I would stiffen up, almost in a panic, and angrily wriggle out of her grip like a feral cat, fighting to free myself. I would demand that she let me go, and eventually, she

would give up, realizing it was a lost battle. But for me, th
wasn't about bonding. Her arms, tightly restraining me,
feel trapped, and the rocking was meant to lull me to sleep, something I resisted at all costs. Because our Pentecostal beliefs focused
heavily on the supernatural, I misinterpreted my various anxiety-in-
duced issues such as sleep apnea, sleep paralysis, and sleepwalking
as demonic activity. What child willingly relinquishes control of her
eyelids when she has been warned that a devil with pitchfork and
horns is lurking in her room, waiting to harm her?

It was about this age that I first discovered my rose-colored
glasses and what a gift they were! Amidst all my fears, I was promised
that everything happens for a reason and that being grafted into the
Hoffmann vine was no random accident. It wasn't because we were
bad children or because Dean and Lillie were unfit parents. There
was a more comforting and satisfying explanation when looking at
our situation through my special lenses: God did it! Just as Joseph
had been thrown into the pit and sold as a slave to the Egyptians,
to save his family later from starvation, so too God had a special
plan for Jules and me. Our situation didn't need to make sense. It
needed no explanation. All I needed to do was simply trust Jesus.
With my new special lens, I could see myself as the center of the
universe with God moving the players and pawns for my personal
benefit. I needn't lament the loss of my birth family nor resist the love
of the Hoffmanns. I was exactly where I was supposed to be. While
my subconscious continued to work through the trauma, for the next
several years, at least externally, I could finally settle into my permanent and forever family with assurance that I was meant to be there
and that God had everything under control. Putting a happy spin on
confusing and unsettling reality was the beginning of a lifetime of
distorted thinking. When there is an invisible deity in the mix, there's
no longer a level playing field and the tools one uses to weigh choices
become useless. God trumps reason and logic every time.

5

The B-I-B-L-E

"The B-I-B-LE, yes, that's the book for me. I stand alone on the Word of God, the B-I-B-L-E!" This wasn't just a catchy tune I sang every week in Sunday school. No. This was gospel truth. The Bible contained *the* very words of God. I remember owning a small children's Bible that resided on my wooden nightstand next to my lamp. On Sundays, I earned a gold star for bringing it with me to church, along with my coin offering wrapped in a handkerchief. One evening, when I was supposed to be sleeping, I sat on the floor beside my bed and flipped through the pages of my little Bible, admiring the colored pictures interspersed between the chapters: Adam and Eve, Noah's Ark, Jonah and the Whale, the Nativity, Jesus on the Cross, and the angels at the empty tomb. When Mama peeked her head in the door to check on me, I was sure I was in trouble for not lying down and having my eyes closed. I fully expected to get a spanking. But to my relief, instead, I saw sheer joy on her face, and she quickly slipped away to share with Daddy what she had "caught" me doing. I knew I had made her happy, and so I tried to repeat the behavior as often as possible, making her proud of me for showing interest in this very special book, even though I was too young to read the pages. After returning from church camp, at age nine, I got my first big-kid, red-letter edition as a gift from Mama, and inscribed inside the cover, she penned these words: "Dear Joy, always remember, this book will keep you from sin, but sin will also keep you from reading this book." This warning was so simple yet profound, and I took her words to be as inerrant as the good book itself. I knew The Holy Bible contained the words to eternal life and I needed to heed its message. I also knew that if I didn't read it and follow its teachings, I would be damned to hell, so I held the Bible in highest regard.

My infallible holy guidebook provided the blueprint for how everything in the entire universe was made. God did it! From the Creation story in Genesis, I learned that God made the whole world in six days by speaking it into existence. And at the end of each creative masterpiece, God proudly declared, "It is good!" Once, in Sunday school, my teacher asked, "Who made the trees?" The class chanted in unison, "God!" "Who made the moon and stars? "God!" Who made people and flowers?" "God!" Who made the air we breathe and the water we drink? "God!" God made every plant and animal in the universe and every planet, star, and constellation. To every question related to existence, the answer was "God! God! God!" I secretly questioned this idea when I knew things like houses, clothes, cars, and toys were made by people and not the result of a "Let there be" voice command from heaven but simply tucked away the exceptions so that my "truth" could remain uncontested. My unwavering allegiance to a God who could break all the rules; appear to be evil, even though he was good; become frustrated and powerless, despite his omnipotence; and defy the very laws of the universe that he created kept me locked into a magical world, where reason, logic, and critical thinking were not only useless but completely unnecessary. It didn't even occur to me to question a story involving a talking snake, a magic fruit and flying angels. Of course it was true, not because it was rational but because my God could do anything!

Within my belief system, not only was there a God who was always watching, judging, and ready to throw me in hell for the most minor of offenses such as saying *fart*, there was also a malevolent force at work, trying to tempt me to sin. Many children have unreasonable fears of monsters who purportedly lurk under the bed or hide in the shadowy umbrella of night. But thoughtful parents typically alleviate their young one's fears by assuring them that they are completely safe and that the boogeyman doesn't exist. They may put a night light in their room or sing them lullabies to help them fall asleep. In my brand of Christianity, however, it was the opposite. We were warned that there indeed was an evil presence watching our every move and constantly looking for an opportunity to strike. This embodiment of evil was intent on destroying us every hour of every day, and we needed to always be on our guard. For us, the threat was real and was even reinforced in sermons. Apart from religion, if any parent ever dared to terrorize their kids by convincing him or her that the imaginary demons hiding in their closet were, in fact, real and that their distress was justified, they would have social workers or mental health specialists knocking on their door. And yet no one seemed alarmed that I believed in a supernatural villain named Satan and his minions, who were out to get me. He was described in the Bible as a roaring lion, roaming around, seeking people to devour. This crafty foe could also play dirty tricks on me or even cause harm by making my bicycle brakes suddenly stop working, for example. Much like a naughty leprechaun turning children's milk green on St. Patty's Day, he was blamed for everything, from flat tires and electricity blackouts, to the cows getting out of the fenced pasture. The bad news was that I was in constant danger of this unseen predator. My natural response was fear and a sense of helplessness.

Like other good fundamentalists, I spent my youth interpreting current events, politics, and war in the context of the supernatural, jumping on the bandwagon of every wild conspiracy theory implicating Lucifer and promising a deliverer, Jesus. In my lifetime, Henry Kissinger, the Reverend Sun Myung Moon, Ronald Reagan, Mikhail Gorbachev, and even Pope Benedict XVI were accused of being the Antichrist, with no apologies offered for defamation of character, when no horns ever sprouted and the allegations proved unfounded. Later some proclaimed, with convincing zeal, that the Antichrist wasn't a person but a thing. Hence the giant computer in Belgium named the Beast, became a likely suspect, powered by the demons themselves to usher in Armageddon. Procter and Gamble products were boycotted because the logo used was interpreted as Satanic. Rock music purportedly had secret demonic messages imbedded, when the records were played backward. In my world, this wasn't just Hollywood sci-fi with special effects. This was the real deal, and I was truly terrified.

But then came King Jesus on his white horse, to the rescue. This was the "Good News!" He promised to protect me, but only if I was obedient and stayed close to him. If I wandered away from the fold, I would be an open target. And if I had enough faith, I could even fight the devil myself with special weapons of warfare: a breastplate of righteousness, sword of truth, and helmet of salvation. The joy, joy, joy, joy, down in my heart was in response to the fact that God had provided a big brother to walk alongside me and effectively beat up my enemy for me. With fear and threat of harm as the backdrop, Christianity became wonderful news.

Still, in my heart of hearts, I had a hard time trusting God, though I never would have admitted it out loud. That would be like declaring, "The Emperor has no clothes." My secret mistrust found its roots in the creation story. I knew what I was supposed to think—that God loved Adam and Eve, but they sinned, forcing God to punish them. But for the life of me, I couldn't understand why on earth—literally "on earth"—God made Satan in the first place. If in the beginning, everything God made was good and perfect, why was Satan there, and why did God let him have so much free reign in his perfect garden *and* in the whole world? The creation story did not paint a comforting picture of God helping or defending or protecting his creation. He made a tree with delicious fruit, put it right smack in the middle of the garden, told Adam and Eve not to eat it, sent Satan to tempt them, hid in the shadows, and watched, never once intervening, *let* them be deceived, and then punished them afterward for disobeying. Inwardly, I viewed God as a trickster, always trying to test my faith to see if I was worthy of his love. Inwardly, I feared I would fail the test. But outwardly, I boldly proclaimed victory in Jesus and sang militant songs about stomping on the devil's head and marching in the Lord's army.

6

I'm No Kin to the Monkey, No No No!

As I grew older, the indoctrination continued, and layer by layer, my spiritual foundation was deepening. Heaven, hell, angels, demons, God, Satan, miracles, new birth, Jesus, and the supernatural became the brick and mortar that defined my world view, with the Holy Bible as my cornerstone. My brainwashing was so complete that the idea of evolution, when presented to me at age eleven, didn't even have a fighting chance. Darwin was synonymous with the Devil, and the entire theory was summed up as yet another crazy, sinister plot by Satan to try and convince humans that they descended from monkeys. Jerry Falwell, a prominent TV evangelist, warned parents to protect their children from this evil propaganda being taught in our government schools. Of course, in my mind, *everybody* knew evolution was false. The Bible was the authority on the subject, and it said Adam came from mud that God shaped into a person and then animated by breathing into his nostrils. Then Eve started out as a rib bone but magically turned into a woman—a much more plausible notion, in my mind than (eye roll) evolving from monkeys, which ironically, as we know, wasn't even an accurate view of evolution in the first place! For several weeks on his Sunday broadcast, Robin and Crystal, two young girls who could harmonize flawlessly, entertained the congregation with an anti-evolution song, which Falwell encouraged Christian youngsters to learn to counter the lies they might hear from their teachers. The catchy little song was called "I'm No Kin to the Monkey." And of course, my sister and I learned every verse and proudly sang along, truly believing that we were arming ourselves with the best ammunition ever to refute this evil teaching.

I'm No Kin to the Monkey
Dr. Theron Babcock

I'm no kin to the monkey, no no no,
The monkey's no kin to me, yeah yeah yeah,
I don't know much about his ancestors,
But mine didn't swing from a tree.

It seems so unbelievable,
And yet they say that it's true,
They're teaching us about it in school now,
That humans were monkeys once too.

Chorus
Although it's so ridiculous,
They're teaching us now that it's true,
The teachers that came from a monkey,
Would be better off in a zoo.

Chorus
It seems so much more believable,
And surely, surely it's true,
That God made Man in His image,
No monkey story will do.

Chorus
This monkey business has to go,
Because it just isn't true,
It's such a disgrace to the monkey,
A disgrace to the human race too.

Oooo, I'm no kin to the monkey, no no no,
The monkey's no kin to me, yeah yeah yeah,
I don't know much about his ancestors,
But mine didn't swing from a tree,
Mine didn't swing from a tree,
Mine didn't swing from a tree.

And that was all it took for me to reject evolution; A preacher on TV (who wouldn't lie) told me evolution was false because it didn't line up with the Bible, and kids sang a clever song, poking fun at it. Touché'! No thinking or questioning required. Who dunnit? God dunnit. And that was that.

7

This Little Piggy Cried, Wah, Wah, Wah

"God is a miracle-working God! Can I get an amen?"

"Amen!" I would scream! I believed all the Bible stories—blind men and lepers and cripples, oh, my!—all healed by Jesus. And week after week, people stood up and testified that they too had been healed of one thing or another—usually ailments not visible with the naked eye; nonetheless, I was convinced God was still in the miracle-working business. So one Sunday night, when the pastor told the congregation that he had a word from the Lord that people were gonna be healed, "*glory-da-god,*" I eagerly anticipated *my* first miracle.

The year prior, my sister and I had been playing chase in the yard while Mama was cutting the grass. Jules ran directly in front of the gas push mower as I followed close behind in hot pursuit. I'm not sure how I fell, but the next thing I knew, I was lying on the ground with both feet caught in the whirling blades and screaming in terror as Mama immediately killed the motor and pulled the machine away in a state of fluster and panic. "Jules, go get your brothers!" Mama ordered. "Bring towels!" Within seconds, my three brothers and the women who had been practicing a choral piece for church rushed out of the house, rehearsal immediately suspended, as they helped wrap my bloody feet for transport to the hospital. The soprano and alto section prayed loudly in tongues while Ray swiftly carried me to the car and perched me on Mama's lap. Though my toes were badly cut, some hanging by a thread, my heavy-duty leather Buster Brown shoes, tenderized from the blades like a dog's old chew toy, had saved the day as they protected them from becoming pulverized. Daddy, with his grease-stained coveralls, came barreling from the repair shop, diagonal from the house, scolding and berating Mama before she was even within earshot. He jumped in the driver's seat, and pumped with adrenaline, veered almost out of control from one side of the ditch to the other on the gravel road leading into town while I repeatedly wailed, "I don't want to die, I don't want to go to heaven!"

"What in tarnation is the matter with you!" Daddy barked accusatorily at Mama. "For cryin' out loud! I'll tell you one thing for sure, you ain't never touching the lawn mower again! What was you thinkin'? I know what you was thinkin'! You wasn't thinkin'! That's what you was doin'! You was thinkin' 'bout everything *but* mowing the good-fer-nothin' yard. Why, I have half a mind to . . ." On and on he ranted, spewing judgment and hateful criticism on Mama, at times, not even making any sense as his name calling sounded more like random words on a magnetic poetry wall: "knuckle-headed," "don't know feet from a pile of you-know-what," "I hope you learnt your lesson real good!" With tears pouring down her face and caressing me in her lap, Mama tried to ignore his insults while calmly assuring me that I wasn't going to die. When we arrived at the hospital, a man with scissors promptly cut off my pants, and I remember feeling embarrassed and exposed to be in a public place in just my underwear, a fate almost as horrendous as having my bloody toes dangling like worms on a fishing line. Thankfully every digit was saved, even though they were badly damaged and would remain forever disfigured.

While it was one of the scariest events for me, it was also clearly one of the most regretful moments for my dear mama, who felt responsible even though she was clearly not to blame. How could she have anticipated that I would trip and fall right in front of her? I'm sure she replayed the scenario like a broken record, wondering if she could have done anything differently to prevent the accident. Despite the instant replays in her mind, she couldn't turn back the clock and make my feet whole again. And then there was my sister, Jules, who had to watch visitors come over bringing me "Get well" presents such as teddy bears, coloring books, and crayons while she was often blindly ignored because her ten toes happened to be intact. Mama bought a beautiful new red Radio Flyer wagon for me to ride in until one of my feet healed enough for me to get around on crutches. I got to be the poor "crippled" princess being pulled around in my shiny red carriage, evoking sympathy, while Jules, by default, was given the role of thankless grunt horse, bitterly leading the parade. Everyone, for different reasons, was eager for me to heal and move on.

A year later, Pastor Pete, our old skinny pastor with slicked-back gray hair and beady eyes, retrieved his anointing oil from his weathered gray suit pocket and invited people to come forward while the spirit was moving. I thought about my crippled toes and wondered if God had me in mind when he talked to Pastor Pete. With my childlike faith, I whispered to my mama, "I would like to go up for prayer." Mama seemed surprised and asked me if I was sure. There was a hint of doubt in her voice as if she were thinking, "Oh crap. She's calling his bluff. What do I do?" When I insisted, she reluctantly obliged, and we went hand in hand to the altar, where I stood in the center of a circle surrounded by a forest of tall legs. Many hands were placed on my head and shoulders while the other hands shot up in the air, like a radio antennae, receiving a heavenly signal. The pastor dabbed oil on my forehead, and the deacons began to speak in tongues and plead for a healing. "In the name of Jeee-sus, we command Joy's toes to be healed. "Yes, Hallelujah! Heal this little girl's feet!" "We rebuke the enemy and claim a total healing!" "Sho ko ron do la la la ma shee ra!" The congregation extended their hands toward the altar as well, adding their supplications to the cacophony. The pleadings ended, and Pastor Pete told me to take off my shoes, but before I did, he offered a quick disclaimer, to cover his bases, in the event of a less than desirable outcome. "If God chooses not to heal you this time, Joy, it's b'coz he wants to use your accident to teach you a lesson or to encourage someone else who might be sufferin', *glory-da-god*!" "Yes! Praise Jeeesus!" the faithful echoed.

Nervously, I began to unlace my shoes, hoping desperately that God didn't want to "teach me a lesson" but instead that the magic oil, prayers, and jibber-jabber had worked. As I slowly pulled off my socks, I held my breath in suspense, thinking about what this miracle would mean for Mama and me. All the guilt and shame she needlessly carried would be instantly erased, and I could go back to wearing the cute buckle shoes again instead of the ugly lace-ups that offered more room but betrayed the current fads. When the unveiling was complete, I looked down to see the same damaged toes that had carried me to the altar. To my dismay, there was no evidence that God had intervened. No healing. No miracle.

When I got home, I remembered Pastor Pete's words and resigned myself to the fact that God *needed* my toes to be mangled for reasons unknown to me and that was that. When we prayed, I was told that God either says, "yes," "no," or "not yet." How convenient. So regardless the outcome of prayer, I could still affirm that God could be trusted even though my request for healing was denied. Since the answer was clearly not "yes," I held out hope that it was not a definitive "no" either, examining my toes very carefully for months, looking for signs of improvement and at times tricking my mind into thinking they looked a tiny bit better. One time, Jules cut my doll's hair, promising it would grow back. I could've sworn it was longer each day, but after a year or so (ever the optimist), when the bangs were still little stubs next to the scalp, I finally accepted the painful truth that I had been regretfully mistaken and so it was with my toes. As a trusting child, I dutifully praised God anyway, thanking him for hearing my prayer even though it wasn't the answer I had wanted.

8

Deviled Eggs and Sinner's Prayer

Ron, the second eldest of my big brothers, was the first to marry, when Jules and I were about seven. His bride, Rosalie, came from a staunch Mennonite community a few miles down the road and, though friendly, was a stickler for rules. I often got the impression that she did not approve of our manners, and I'm sure she was justified in her critique, as we were often accused of being "born in a barn," no offense to Jesus. One day, while visiting, she had prepared something in the kitchen, and for the life of me I can't say for certain what it was. One part of my brain remembers deviled eggs. Another part imagines cupcakes. Since it doesn't matter, let's just go with deviled eggs because that seems most fitting for a conversion story. When Rosalie came into the kitchen later, she noticed the deviled eggs had been de-shuffled as if someone had been carelessly tampering with them. Her meticulous rows looked like the messy cacophony of folding chairs in the gym after a school play. For a person who liked order, this was cause for alarm, and immediately, the interrogation began. "Joy! What happened to my deviled eggs? Who was messing with them?" she asked accusatorily. I assured her emphatically that I had not. Feeling defensive that I had been wrongly accused, I tried to explain, "I saw Sammy [our Siamese cat] pounce on the counter and swat them with his paw. I tried to shoo him off," I offered weakly. She didn't believe me for a second. "Sammy did not jump on the counter!

33

You are lying! This is something you did, isn't it?" Again, I denied any culpability, sticking with "The cat did it!" despite her attempts at wearing me down and forcing a confession. To be fair, I was a filthy, no-good liar at age seven and had probably given Rosalie good reason to doubt my sincerity. But this time, I was telling the *God-honest* truth, and she wouldn't believe me. Contemplating her next move, she called my faith into question. "Are you even a Christian, Joy?" she demanded. "Have you asked Jesus into your heart?" She awaited my response with smug, condescending satisfaction, as if she knew what my answer would be.

How dare Rosalie accuse me of not being a Christian! "Yes! Of course I've asked Jesus into my heart!" I blurted almost too forcefully, feigning righteous indignation. The truth was, I hadn't. In that moment, I realized that I had never recited the sinner's prayer, and I couldn't believe I had overlooked such an important detail after having been in church already for four years of my young life. But I certainly couldn't admit it to Rosalie. She would use it as confirmation that her assessment of my lack of credibility was justifiably warranted and I would forever have to take the rap for the goddamn eggs. So in order to prove that I was not a liar, I . . . well . . . umm . . . lied. And yes, I do see the irony of it. Immediately, I secretly made a beeline to my room, knelt beside my bed, and retroactively asked Jesus into my heart, and as a first order of business, begged him to forgive me for fibbing about it earlier. I'm still not sure if that even counted, but it was my first of many "Come to Jesus" meetings over the next several years. I went to the altar nearly every Sunday to "Get right with Jesus" because I had stolen envelopes from mama's stationery drawer, tattled on my sister, only *pretended* to practice the piano, or sampled fistfuls of sugar from the pantry while Mama had been napping. But no matter how many times I went forward, I never truly felt different. I always left church the very same way I had entered, except for the puffy eyes from my tearful repentance. I had no assurance whatsoever that God loved me or that he wanted me to go to heaven when I died, especially when crafty old Satan was on the loose, vying for my soul through deception. I felt that all the pressure was on me to stop sinning and that wasn't possible, even though I was *promised* a new heart that was capable of obeying Jesus when I accepted him as my savior. I was taught that when someone becomes a Christian, he becomes a brand-new person inside. The old is gone and the new has come. Yet I still sinned, evidence that I might not have a new and improved heart after all. Therefore, I secretly wondered if God had, in fact, heard my prayers.

Doubts regarding my own salvation stemmed largely from a theological belief called *predestination* that our church taught. We believed that our eternal fate had already been determined and could not be changed. Before we were ever born, God knew who would accept him and who wouldn't and our lives would simply play out to the already predetermined outcome. Even though God foreknew who would choose him, his hands were tied because of free will. How could I possibly know if I had been predestined or not? No matter how many times I repented for my sins, I couldn't be assured that I would die with every sin accounted for. God could not allow sin in his presence, and if I had even one bad attitude before taking my final breath, I could be separated from Him forever. Jesus said, "If your eye offends you, pluck it out. Better to throw one eye into the fire than have your whole body burn in hell" (Matthew 18:9). I remember lying awake many nights, kneeling beside my bed and literally begging God amidst fearful sobs, "Please let me go to heaven! Please, Jesus! Even if I'm supposed to go to hell, please write my name in your book! Please! I don't want to go to hell!" I asked him to forgive every sin I would ever commit in advance just to make sure I had covered all my bases. Still my poor young psyche was wracked with unrelenting fear. When I was in the fifth grade, I encountered my first glimmer of hope.

My Sunday school teacher, Sister Isaac, a beautiful woman from England with a lovely Mary Poppins kind of demeanor, let us in on a special secret. She told us (spoken in a proper British accent), "God won't let people burn in hell for-ev-eh. Instead, after suffering for a time, we would either be set free or simply cease to exist." This was great news! I mean, it was still terrible news but at least not as horrendous as eternal conscious torment. My hopes were short-lived, however, when I reported this enlightening insight to my parents on the car ride home. "That is not true!" Mama shouted sternly. "Your teacher is not following the Bible. It's appointed unto man *once* to die, and after that, the judgment. There are no second chances!" Any hope of escaping my fiery destiny, should my name be missing from the Lamb's Book of Life, was shattered, and I was back to crying myself to sleep in my pillow, in dreaded anguish.

9

Make Love to Jesus

A turning point in my "walk with the Lord" happened the summer I went to church camp in Bellevue, Idaho, situated just minutes from the famous Sun Valley ski resort and Ketchum, the resting place of Ernest Hemingway. It was there that I had a spiritual encounter that changed my life. The documentary *Jesus Camp* paints a vivid portrait of what my experiences were like. We started our day with devotions in our cabin led by our camp counselor, followed by breakfast and then immediately to chapel, where we sang kid-friendly action songs, like "Hallelu-hallelu-hallelu-hallelujah, Praise ye the Lord." The boys would stand and shout at the top of their lungs the Hallelu's, and then the girls, not wanting to be outdone, would jump up and scream their part, "Praise ye the Lord." We basically had church morning, noon, and night for the entire week. In the evenings, we dressed up and headed to the big tent revival, where the children's pastor pulled out all the stops and offered an emotional appeal that one simply couldn't refuse. Each night for a week, there was music, skits, and powerful object lessons to drive home the message being conveyed. Some pastors used puppets. Others used magic tricks. One lady, as I recall, had a dog who could howl specific notes when she heard them being played on the piano. "Muffy is singing a B to remind you to go to Sunday School." What the hell? Even we knew *B* should've been for "*Be*-lieve on the Lord Jesus Christ" and *G* should've been for "*Go* to Sunday school." Needless to say, there were some evangelists who were better than others. Still, regardless the medium, the message was always the same: You are a sinner, doomed to hell. Jesus is the solution and you need to invite him into your heart *now*. If you wait, you might die and burn in hell F-O-R-E-V-E-R . . . ever . . . ever . . . ever (reverb).

It was in such a meeting that I was convinced that Jesus was calling me to walk down the aisle to the altar. This wasn't just a call to salvation but an invitation to be filled with the Holy Ghost. I had prayed the sinner's prayer hundreds of times since the "deviled egg" incident. I had also prayed to be filled with the Holy Spirit numerous times, but to no avail. My spiritual language never came. I couldn't understand why God would keep this gift from me, when He Himself had promised, "Ask and you will receive." But this time was different. The pastor said, "If your heart is beating heavily, that is the Holy Spirit knocking on your door. He's inviting you to come forward and be saved and baptized with the Spirit." My heart was pounding out of my chest. "He *must* be talking to me!" In almost a trance-like state, I made my way to the front and was met by a counselor who directed me to kneel.

As I began to sob loudly (that seemed to be the prerequisite for receiving the Holy Spirit), the counselor, praying for me, encouraged me to lift my hands and just start worshipping Jesus, telling him how much I loved him. Then she offered some syllables for me to try. Say, "Shan-da-la-ma-sha-ku-rah." I copied her. She was pleased. She repeated the sounds several times as I mimicked her like a talking parrot, careful to match her sounds as closely as possible. She then told me, "Just relax and let the Spirit do the talking." My teeth started to chatter, as if standing in the middle of a snowstorm, waiting for the school bus. "Good! Just let it go," the counselor encouraged. The teeth chatters turned into "lalalalalalala." "That's right, sweetie. Make love to Jesus," she said over and over. *Ewwwww!* I shuddered to myself, blushing in preadolescent embarrassment. I couldn't even say the word *sex* without turning fifty shades of red, so the imagery of becoming physically "intimate" with Jesus was horrifying. Still I pressed on until my la-la-la-la's reached a feverish *climax*—pun intended—accompanied by orgasmic groans from my mentor. "Yes! Yes! Oh, yes! That's right!" I had worked myself into such an emotional frenzy I couldn't tell if God was manipulating my tongue or if it was just my own hysteria talking. All doubts were erased, though, when she assured me I had indeed received my heavenly love language. I guess she would know, right? She *was* the counselor, after all. I was convinced that I had finally been "touched" by God. I want to say "molested," but I fear I am taking the metaphor a little too far. This was the evidence I needed to trust that He loved me, heard my prayers, and knew me personally. I was elated. The Holy Ghost was going to keep me from sinning so that I wouldn't go to hell. What a relief! This time, I believed I truly was a new creation. The old me had died and the new me had just been born. Unlike my previous attempts at salvation, this time I knew I was born-again and spirit filled, and I vowed to live the rest of my life for Jesus. The nagging fear of going to hell finally dissipated as I basked in the indescribable joy of knowing that the creator of the universe knew me personally and had called me out to be his disciple. What utter relief and pure delight. I no longer needed to "prove" myself to God. He assured me that I belonged to him. My heart had never felt so light and free.

On the final evening, after we had bawled our eyes out for a week, draining the reservoir of tears reserved for repentant sinners, and hoarse from all the screaming "I LOVE YOU, JESUS! I LOVE YOU, LORD!" at the top of our lungs, in that feverish, altered state of euphoria, we then went outside the revival tent and gathered around a large bonfire. This was the culminating event to seal the deal and send us back to our homes and schools and churches, on fire for Jesus and ready to change our world. We dipped our stick in the fire, watching the embers burn at the end, while we sang, reverently, Kurt Kaiser's hit, "Pass it On."

> It only takes a spark to get a fire going, and soon
> all those around can warm up in its glowing.
> That's how it is with God's love, once you've
> experienced it. You spread his love to everyone,
> you want to pass it on.

My heart was bursting with joy. I wanted to be a light in the darkness. I wanted to be the salt of the earth. The reservoir was filling up again, and suddenly, I had yet another pool of tears to shed. Gently, while a guitarist was playing softy in the background, "Just as I Am," the pastor told a story about a former camper who stood around a fire just like the one we were encircling. He told about the boy's rebellion and how he was unwilling to give up his sinful pleasures and follow Jesus. He talked about how kids, one by one, were throwing their cigarettes and Beatles albums into the fire, but the boy wouldn't budge. He said he wasn't ready but maybe he would get right with God next year. Then the very next day, on the way home from camp, he was in a car accident and . . ."

A hush fell over the camp. We hung on every word as if he were telling one of those suspenseful ghost stories with a dramatic *boo*! at the end. He finished his sentence, ". . . was killed instantly." (There was a long silence.) "Look around!" he continued. "Look at each face. Never again will each of you be together like this. There are no guarantees of how long we will live, and as sure as I'm standing here tonight, one of you will probably die before camp next year. Are you ready to meet Jesus? Are you willing to let go of whatever sin you are hiding? Come on! Throw it in the bonfire! Let it go! Get right with God!" One by one the sticks were tossed into the purifying blaze, along with a collection of paraphernalia that students had gathered from their personal stash of contraband, amidst hugging and still *more* weeping. As I released my stick into the fire, I made a promise to Jesus that I would be sold out to him and follow him with every fiber in my being, and I truly meant it.

10

Alien Invasion

A couple of months after my mountaintop experience at camp, I entered sixth grade, on fire for Jesus and ready to change the world. Sixth grade can be a tumultuous time for many kids, and my experience was no different. With the onset of puberty, raging hormones, acne, and the insatiable need for social acceptance, it's no wonder I have no desire to revisit 1974 even if my time machine could take me back with just the simple push of a button. To compound an already difficult stage of development, my Christian zeal only added to the awkwardness. During Bible camp, I was warned that there was a cost to taking up my cross and following Jesus. I was told that I would be hated, ridiculed, alienated, and rejected for being a Christian but the payoff in heaven would be worth it all. When I threw my stick in the purging bonfire on the last evening, I was essentially saying that I accepted the challenge. From that decision emerged a recurring theme, one that ran contrary to my natural instincts. Just at the crucial time when my greatest social need was to fit in, the Bible said the opposite. "Christians *don't* belong here on earth. We are merely sojourners passing through on our way to our heavenly home, with streets of gold and a mansion awaiting us on arrival," my pastor repeated often. Consequently, I entered sixth grade, bracing myself to be an outcast and even purposely alienating myself from the group at times to prove my allegiance to Jesus. While the other kids were busy passing notes back and forth and gossiping about who had a crush on whom and who was going steady with whom, I was busy obsessing about "winning the lost." Moreover, while the others were blabbering on about their heartthrob Donnie Osmond and cooing over the adorable Michael Jackson, I was memorizing Bible passages and constantly searching for signs that other kids shared my passion for truth. But most of the students didn't give spiritual matters a second thought. They were too busy telling dirty jokes and bragging about their sexual exploits like getting to "second base," a metaphor I only pretended to comprehend. There were two kids besides Jules and myself who grew up in the Pentecostal church, but even they showed absolutely no hint of being saved. Both had come from dysfunctional homes, with histories of substance abuse and multiple divorces, further tainting their already-incestuous family tree. The Mormon kids shared some of my zeal, but I was told they were a cult, so I couldn't identify with them, either; though, oddly enough, our beliefs were very similar. While this year marked a time of self-discovery for others, I was practicing self-denial. "Christ must increase, but I must decrease." Christianity was about dying to self and resisting temptation.

Chuck, the new kid on the block (funny how his name so perfectly fit the stereotype), with long blond hair and bangs in his face, was the boy every girl fought over. Apart from the unsightly plaque on his teeth, he was otherwise a perfect specimen, wooing hearts and then breaking them left and right with promises of going steady, followed by the terrible breakup a week later. I must confess that I too had a slight crush on Chuck, but I certainly never admitted it because I had bigger issues to worry about—namely, the rapture. The traveling evangelists and TV preachers prophesied that Jesus was due for his second coming before 1980 at the latest, and so I couldn't just relax, have fun, live a little, and then make a deathbed confession later. Oh, no, no, no. Rapture preparedness was a 24/7 endeavor.

I remember at times, in the winter, retreating to the less-trodden area of the playground and writing messages like "Jesus Loves You" in the snow, hoping that someone would come along later, read it, and get saved. To my dismay, however, not a single convert, to my knowledge, was ever made due to my proselytizing on the white canvas.

11

A Test of Faith

For a few months, we had a young, vibrant student teacher, who happened to be a peace-loving, tie-dyed, granola-eating hippie with Birkenstocks on her feet to complete the image. The most scandalous news about her was that she, a white female, was "shacking up" with a (hushed whisper) black man. I'm not sure what was worse: that she was having sex outside of marriage or that she was in a racially "mixed" relationship, but the rumor mill had a heyday in our small conservative town while she was there. Nonetheless, the students were crazy about her because she was interesting and liked to think outside the box. One day, she announced that each of us had to dance our way into the lunch line. Dancing was considered the *D* word in my circle and definitely a "su'um we don't do." It was strictly forbidden in my church, along with smoking, drinking, going to theatres or pool halls, using face cards, shaking dice, wearing red lipstick or red nail polish, working on Sunday, listening to secular music, and even mixed bathing (sharing the swimming pool with the opposite sex). Everyone else in the class giggled and started dancing their way into the line, even the Mormons. But I knew I couldn't partake. I was an *alien*, answering to a higher call. I had made a vow to God that I wouldn't participate in "worldly" pleasures. So awkwardly, I stayed defiantly unmoved in my seat with my "Smile, Jesus loves you" patch sewn securely on my coat jacket for emphasis. When the last student had finally joined the group, the teacher noticed that I hadn't budged. Puzzled, she asked why I wasn't dancing, and I informed her, in a pious yet hushed tone, that dancing was against my religion. "Against your what?" she asked, incredulously. "My religion," I repeated, enunciating the words as if talking to a speaker of another language. "How could moving your body be against your religion?" she asked rhetorically, shrugging her shoulders. The entire class looked back at me with puzzled stares. I could feel my cheeks getting hot as I fought valiantly to hold back the tears. Shaking her head in silent resignation, she motioned me to "just get in line." I knew I had disappointed her. The class continued to follow my movements with a mixture of pity and mocking condescension as I quietly made my way to form the caboose, without so much as a hint of any gyrating.

My humiliation engulfed me until I got home and shared with Mama what had happened. Suddenly, my soul welled up with pride as I was deemed a hero for standing up for my faith while my heathen teacher was villainized for inviting students into her evil little web of free love and debauchery. One would think she had forced us all into prostitution by the way she was so harshly criticized by Mama. But what truly mattered was that I had pleased God by my act of civil disobedience and I learned to equate embarrassment with spiritual maturity. The more I stood out as "different" and the more I alienated myself from my popular culture, I knew I was identifying with my citizenship in heaven. There was a catchy tune, written by Tom T. Hall, that my hillbilly cousins from Texas taught me, when they came for a visit. It was called "Me 'n Jesus," which became my personal anthem:

> Me n' Jesus, we got our own thing going,
> Me n' Jesus, got it all worked out.
> Me 'n Jesus got our own thing going.
> We don't need anybody
> To tell us what it's all about.

My special God glasses numbed the pain of not fitting in. Instead, they showed me I had something far more valuable than temporary friendships or accolades from mere mortals. I had the creator of the universe on my side, and He promised never to leave me nor forsake me. One day, we would get to dance on fluffy cloud play harps together for all eternity. (Sigh . . . yay.)

I look back to this time with deep sadness, realizing I had been denied a basic human need in the name of pleasing an emotionally abusive god who demanded I feel humiliated and alienated as a test of my allegiance. This is toxic religion at its very core.

12

Deliver Me from My Enemies, Namely, Judy

From the age of three, I had been taught that God looks after his children. If we were ever in a pinch, his winged warriors would come to our rescue, doing battle against the evil forces seeking to cause us harm. I had heard a litany of tales about God heroically diverting disaster or miraculously intervening in a moment of crisis or peril. So in a naively optimistic way, I was like Mr. Magoo, just blindly meandering through life, fully expecting that God had my back. Consequently, it came as quite a shock when a robust Native American bully named Judy accosted me in the school parking lot at recess one day. The Fort Hall Reservation was nearby, but only a handful of kids attended our public school, and Judy was one of them. We referred to them as Indians because political correctness wasn't a thing in the '70s. Racial profiling, however, was. "Everyone" knew that people on the Reservation were lazy alcoholics who liked to start fights and pull out their knives on occasion in our city park. I had heard that they had been given free land, free housing, and free food from the government but were ungrateful and just squandered their resources on booze. So subconsciously, I'm sure I regarded Judy with the same level of disdain that my parents and society did. It stands to reason, then, that I exhibited no charitable instincts to do her any favors, such as share my answers on the States and Capitals test, even though she waved her threatening fist in my face when the teacher wasn't looking, demanding I offer her a glance at my paper. Additionally, I felt the loose change I had found on the snow slope, one day, at recess, while sledding was subject to the rule "finders, keepers," even though she insisted I hand it over to her, when she wasn't even the "loser-weeper." With two strikes against me, I was on her hit list and found myself fearfully evading her menacing threats by hiding in the bathroom stall at recess every day with my feet perched on the toilet seat to avoid being spotted. But one afternoon, before I could make it into hiding, she caught me off guard and managed to separate me from the pack like a poor, helpless gazelle being chased down by hungry wolves. She pushed me on the ground in the faculty parking lot and immediately sat on top of me with her large blubbery mass, pinning me to the snowy asphalt and threatening further harm in her deep, throaty voice if I didn't do what she wanted. And of course, as in any good bully story, I was not allowed to tell the teachers or anyone for that matter. Since my memory fails me about the specifics of the assault, I'm tempted to embellish the account, with descriptions of blood squirting from my nose or chunks of my hair cocooned in her fist. But honestly, the only memory that remains is not so much what happened but how I felt—terrified, helpless, vulnerable, unsafe, and trapped. What would Jesus do? "If someone slaps you on the cheek, turn and let them slap the other one as well." Under the circumstances, I wasn't convinced that this was the best protocol, but my fight or flight instincts were temporarily paralyzed under the weight of her body as she sat on me, and so it turns out, I followed Jesus's advice by default. Before crawling off me and letting me go, she warned, "Watch your back because I'm going to beat you up whenever I feel like it." With that, she stood up and walked away, leaving me trembling, sandwiched between the two parked cars that served only to conceal the crime, rather than to offer any sense of protection. Every day thereafter, I found myself apprehensively looking over my shoulder, wondering when and where she would strike again and praying that God would somehow intervene.

Then one Monday morning, Judy didn't show up for school. I breathed a sigh of relief. "No hiding in the stalls for me today." Shortly after the flag salute, Mr. McComber, the principal, whom we affectionately called Mr. McCucumber, came to our classroom and dropped the bombshell. "I have some very sad news," he began. "Judy Pohipe passed away over the weekend from asphyxiation, due to sniffing spray paint." I nearly yelped out a "Praise the Lord!" but immediately caught myself and sat staring in stunned silence as I contemplated what Mr. McCucumber had just announced. My relief turned to shock. *Dead? How could she be dead? She's only twelve! Judy Pohipe is dead!* It didn't seem real. My brain was having trouble processing the words, and so I rolled them around and around on my tongue like working my way to the chocolate center of a Tootsie Pop. Suddenly I felt guilty because a small part of me was still harboring a smidge of happiness that my days of refuge in the girl's lavatory were finally over. I broke the words into letters. D-E-A-D, dead! The song from *The Wizard of Oz* came to mind: "Ding, Dong, the witch is dead, which old witch? The wicked witch." *What does it feel like to be dead?* I wondered. One thing I could infer with a reasonable degree of certainty was that Judy was not a Christian. According to the Bible, this preadolescent girl was burning in hell, just like the rebellious boy the preacher warned about at camp, and would continue to scream and writhe for all eternity. As much as I hated her, as much as I feared her, as much as I wanted her to leave me alone, I certainly didn't want her dead. This was the first time a young person that I knew had died, and I didn't know how to make sense of it. My first Bible passage I ever memorized was John 3:16. "For God so loved the World that he gave his only begotten son, that whosoever believeth in him should not perish, but have everlasting life." But what about Judy? Why didn't he even give her a chance to hear the gospel? Maybe he did! What if it was my fault because I didn't witness to her? Such a burden was inconceivable to bear. There was no way I could take responsibility for Judy's fate. Instead, I had to turn the blame to Judy herself. She *chose* to inhale the spray paint and she *chose* to be a bully, and because God is just, he gave her what her sins deserved. Done. God was off the hook, and I was too. The thought of hell was so disturbing that to accept it as a reality, I had to coat my heart with a nonstick layer of callous indifference to make it seem okay. I couldn't change God's Word or the plan of salvation. What was written was written, and I simply had to conform my own mind and conscience to this inconvenient truth. When looking at the tragedy, I could take the focus off Judy's demise and instead, narcissistically, thank God for delivering *me* from my enemy, just as King David had prayed so many times in the Old Testament Psalms.

Part Two

Adolescence
Mascot for Jesus

13

Let's Talk about Sex

As a Christ follower, the Bible was very clear about "sins of the flesh." Virtually every form of sex outside of marriage, right down to a lustful thought, was considered "dirty." It seemed there were dozens of "wrong" ways to engage in sex (imagine Bubba Gump, only replace shrimp with sex): there was fornication, adultery, lust, masturbation, blow jobs, hand jobs, pornography, prostitution, suggestive language, impure thoughts, flirting, dressing provocatively, seducing, making out, dancing—well, you get the idea—but only one God-sanctioned way: the missionary position, in marriage, between a man and a woman. Period. The chances of slipping up in this area seemed great, and even if I didn't have sex but was merely curious about it, I believed I was guilty of sinning. And for some reason, sexual sin was the worst kind of abomination imaginable, second only to grieving the Holy Spirit, a sin that could never be forgiven. So when my own body started to change from innocent child to "sexually ready" woman without my permission, I was fearful and anxious, to say the least. My childbearing hips started to expand, forcing me out of my girl's size 10 slim pants and making me feel fat even though in reality, I was quite lean. Then suddenly, almost overnight, my see-through blouses were starting to reveal puffy little bulges, signifying the inadequacy of the training bras I had acquired the year before. While most girls would proudly flaunt their new embellishments and brag about their cup size, I tried to conceal my emerging nubbins as if they were unsightly malignant growths. To me, my body was an object of shame. It wasn't to be celebrated. It needed to be subdued lest it be used as a vessel of sexual impurity, and yet I had no control over the metamorphosis ensuing. I wasn't emotionally ready to grow up because of the responsibility it represented for me, not only as a Christian but also as a woman. I was the Bride of Christ and needed to be pure and spotless. Even in the context of marriage, I couldn't imagine anything more disgusting than to take off my clothes in front of another person. If these were signs of growing up, I wanted no part of it. I entertained thoughts of suicide to escape the inevitable, but I could never go through with it because I was so terrified of burning in hell.

My lessons about sex and body shame germinated back as early as three years old, when I crawled up on Daddy's lap, shortly after joining the Hoffmanns, straddling his legs and facing him so I could feel the razor stubble on his chin. There had been allegations that Jules and I had been molested at the Slaters, and so Mama was on high alert for any inappropriate behaviors we might exhibit. I was immediately whisked off and told that I could no longer crawl on Daddy's lap because sitting that way was "nasty." Every time Mama used that word, she implied that the action was vulgar, disgusting, and immensely displeasing to God. While I was too little to understand the significance of being banned from Daddy's lap, the message of shame stayed with me, and I don't recall ever asking to be held or cuddled by him again.

Another time, when I was six, after the lawn mowing accident, I was sitting on the floor with bandaged feet, just bored and daydreaming, since I couldn't walk, and I remember innocently touching myself, as if scratching an itch. The immediate sensation brought pleasure, and so I curiously "scratched" just a little bit longer. Suddenly, Mama's voice broke into my silence. "Joy! Stop that! Shame on you!" Once again, *nasty* was the lingering adjective. Embarrassed, I immediately snapped out of my little trance, pulled my hand away, and started to cry. The creation story with Adam and Eve needing clothing to hide their shame reinforced the idea that our bodies, especially certain parts, were sinful, had to be covered up, and for God's sake, never, ever touched.

I also distinctly remember watching *The Beverly Hillbillies*, and in one episode, a young man was chasing Ellie Mae around the "cement pond." It was meant to be silly and hilarious, yet I was immediately gripped with fear for Ellie Mae, because somewhere in my formation of ideas about men was the idea that they were predators and women needed to resist their advances.

Additionally, one needn't cite a peer-reviewed research study to prove that a girl's relationship with her father impacts her future relationships. I loved my dad and I believed he cared for me, but the way he showed it was atypical. Everyone has his or her own love language. For some, it's giving gifts. For others, it's the expenditure of time. For Daddy, it was tickling—not in a creepy pedophile sort of way. Despite his otherwise gruff and angry nature, he tried to exhibit a playful side with Jules and me. Whenever I got within arm's length of him, his big, thick, grease-stained mechanic's fingers, like small tree trunks, would lunge at me, and I would scream with what he perceived as delight, even though his jovial jabbing caused near bruising. This was the closest thing I had to any physical connection with him, and so I welcomed the pain, knowing it made him happy. While I had permission to give him a hug and kiss his cheek to say goodnight, I don't remember any time in my childhood where he initiated, nor do I remember the words "I love you" ever uttered until well into my adult years. Even at my high school graduation, while others were getting giant bear hugs from their fathers, Daddy shook my hand in the reception line, announcing, "Congratulations, Joy," as if I were a distant niece or family friend. Even though his staunch German roots valued stoicism over demonstrative affection, I still trusted that he loved me. Yet I clearly remember doing cartwheels (metaphorically speaking) to get his attention. I tried to show off my new dresses, new shoes, report cards, and achievement awards. Mama always had to remind him to stop what he was doing and listen to me, and his response was usually summarized in only one unconvincing word, "Yep," uttered before returning to the newspaper or the TV show that had his full attention before I had so rudely interrupted him. I'll never forget, though, the time I told him that I had found some shells while playing, earlier that day near a dry river bed. "Really? Where'd you find them?" he asked, with genuine curiosity.

"Over at Osborne's farm," I replied proudly.

"Let me see 'um," he said. I couldn't believe what I was hearing. Daddy wanted to see the shells I had collected! I was elated. I ran downstairs to my bedroom, raced back up, out of breath and grinning, with pride, as I eagerly opened my fist and unveiled the contents in my palm. He took one look, and with a hint of disgust, said, "I thought you said *shekels*. I don't want to see no shells." He shooed my hand away, as if to say, "Get that worthless shit out of my face." I do realize now why he was so disappointed when I couldn't deliver the ancient Middle Eastern currency as my "show and tell." Admittedly, that would've been way more interesting. But at the time, all I wanted was for him to validate me, and when he didn't, he only reinforced the belief that I was valuable for what I could offer and not for who I was. Without the shekels, I was nothing.

From those brief childhood encounters, my attitudes about sex, self-worth, and relationships with men, were being formed, and as a teen, they were wreaking havoc.

On one hand, I was terrified of the idea of sex. Yet at the same time, I desperately craved to be noticed. I didn't have physical beauty nor was I the life of the party. One of the only ways I perceived that I could be less "rejectable" was by being thin. Jules was always the bigger twin—not disproportioned, just a size or two larger because she was the first-born and was the stronger, stockier built of the two of us. To me, she looked like Shirley Temple with an adorable round face, button nose, nice straight teeth, and perfect eyesight to boot. I, on the other hand, resembled a younger version of Nanny McPhee, with cat-eyed glasses and a crazy, crooked tooth right in the middle of my smile. But because we were twins, even though we had physical differences, for some reason, everyone expected us to be the same size. And since we weren't, I heard people say cruel things about Jules. "Why is she so fat and you so skinny? Doesn't she know when to stop eating?" Mind you, these were grown-ups spewing such hurtful comments, and grown-ups were to be trusted. Through observing this type of prejudice, I inferred that a person's weight was a measure of intrinsic worth. To be thin was deemed virtuous, but to be chubby was a moral flaw. I had surgery on my eyes when I was four to correct my crossed eyes and went to the same eye doctor I had as a baby before being adopted. Dr. Clothier remembered my birth mother, Lillie, and said that she was morbidly obese. Mama would use this information as an explanation for our size variance. "Jules probably takes after her birth mother," she would say, "and someday, you might need to be careful too!" This was one more tidbit to add to my reconstruction of chapter 1. "We were neglected, abandoned and unloved by our first parents. Dean was an alcoholic and child molester, and Lillie was morbidly obese." I had no memory of Lillie, and the one and only nugget I had was that she was overweight. Was she pretty or clever or gentle or funny? It didn't matter. She was sentenced to only one unflattering description. Never mind that she had birthed five children, including *twins*, when the Dr. had made her acquaintance. When my body started to morph, I panicked, thinking, "It's starting! I've been predestined for fatness and there's nothing I can do about it." Just like Oedipus, I tried to outsmart fate. I stopped eating. At the time, I had no idea the psychological implications of *anorexia nervosa* or what triggers such a disorder. All I could internalize was that I wanted to control the effects of my changing body.

After several months, I got thinner and thinner and was getting weaker by the day, but I couldn't stop starving myself. When I looked in the mirror, the bony frame staring back still looked unacceptable, and my self-loathing became obsessive.

Our family eventually moved into town from the country, and we lived just a few blocks from school and four to six blocks from the grocery store. Jules and I would often walk or ride our bikes downtown from our house to pick up some item or ingredient needed for dinner, and we would cut across the city park to save time. One day, my legs gave out, while walking across the park. I would take a few steps, fall down, get up, walk a few more steps, and collapse again. I couldn't seem to keep my balance walking on the uneven grass. Jules was getting concerned, and I begged her not to tell. Then walking to school, the next days and weeks, I had similar struggles. My legs just couldn't seem to hold up my frame. Still my parents didn't notice.

They may have thought I was just going through a growth spurt and were unconcerned with my clumsiness. Finally, one afternoon, Mama and Daddy had gone somewhere, and I was asked to mow the lawn before going to a Friday night football game at the high school. I could barely push the mower. This had been my job for a few years as therapy from getting my toes mangled as a child. To stand behind the mower pushing it, rather than being in its destructive path, helped me overcome my phobia. But this day, I had made only a few laps around the edge of the yard before I blacked out. When I came to, I called for Jules and told her I needed help. She was visibly scared. I honestly don't remember what happened next. I don't know if Jules told Mama or if I did.

I didn't understand that my condition had a name or that the underlying issues causing it—low self-esteem, poor body image, difficulty expressing feelings, rigid thinking patterns, and need for control—described me to a tee. In my ignorance, I believed my mom's assessment: this was a spiritual issue. I had, in fact, been ensnared by the devil. Instead of counseling or a doctor's visit, Mama's solution for me was to simply repent for being vain, rebuke Satan, and to ask Jesus to help me. It was my faith that had reinforced the very feelings that contributed to my eating disorder: self-hatred, suppressed emotions, and narrow, rigid beliefs. But then, ironically, Jesus was conveniently touted as the cure. I am aware now that I was saved because Mama literally force-fed me for a solid year and *not* because I had rebuked "the enemy." But at the time, I could only see what my special glasses wanted me to see: my wretchedness and God's amazing grace. I testified in church many years later that Jesus had "miraculously" set me free from Satan's grip, *Praise the Lord*, even though I had still secretly purged on and off for another five years. I blamed myself for the relapses, knowing Christ was fully willing and able to help me, if only *I* would cooperate. I decided such a disclaimer was not necessary and would only diminish the miracle.

14

Water Baptism

Another step in my faith journey involved the sacrament of water baptism. The scriptures were clear that immersion was a prerequisite for heaven, and with the rapture close at hand, I knew I couldn't procrastinate any longer. For years, I had contemplated it, but the thought of being submerged under water and then pulled out again was unnerving. Every *what if* scenario replayed in my mind. *What if* I get water up my nose? *What if* I swallow water and start choking or coughing? *What if* I panic and accidentally pull the pastor in? If anything *could* go wrong, I was confident it would happen with me because Murphy's Law followed me around like a jealous lover.

But having watched dozens of men, women, and children go before me over the years, my reluctance subsided and I decided to take the plunge. The part that terrified me the most was knowing I had to give my testimony of how Jesus had changed my life prior to getting officially dunked. I broke out in a terrible case of acne from the stress, which only added to the trauma of facing the congregation, shrouded in self-consciousness and zits and declaring weakly my unabashed love for the Lord. Afterwards, I made my way into the baptismal, thinking how ironic it was that my sins were as white as snow and yet my red, splotchy face hinted of leprosy.

When I came out of the water, I had hoped to feel different, sparkly clean inside and out, maybe even miraculously pimple-free, but any spiritual bliss was upstaged by the extra weight I was carrying as the long white angel gown, appropriate for a Christmas pageant, my mama had made for me, seemed to soak up about a gallon of the water from the tank. I labored off stage, sloshing and leaking and dripping all the way to the exit door, where I had to descend a very narrow flight of wooden stairs. The next thing the congregation heard was a *thump, fa-thump, fa-thump, fa-thump fa-thump, fa-thump, bang,* as the slippery steps sent me tumbling downward on every part of my body except for my feet, which somehow managed to find themselves over my head and of little use. The next thing I heard was uproarious laughter: a clear sign the spectators knew what had just transpired behind the wall.

Why couldn't God just send a sweet dove to land on my head to show his favor? Why did he always have to humiliate me? Again, I concluded, that God expected me to identify with the suffering of his son. And so, as I lay at the bottom of the stairs, bruised, embarrassed, and fighting back tears, I could almost hear the voice from heaven saying, "This is my beloved daughter in whom I am well pleased."

15

Preparing for the Rapture

I Wish We'd All Been Ready
Larry Norman

Life was filled with guns and war
And all of us got trampled on the floor
I wish we'd all been ready

The children died, the days grew cold
A piece of bread could buy a bag of gold
I wish we'd all been ready

There's no time to change your mind
The son has come and you've been left behind

A man and wife asleep in bed
She hears a noise and
Turns her head, he's gone
I wish we'd all been ready

Two men walking up a hill
One disappears and
One's left standing still
I wish we'd all been ready

There's no time to change your mind
The son has come and you've been left behind

The father spoke, the demons dined
How could you have been so blind?

There's no time to change your mind
The son has come and you've been left behind
There's no time to change your mind
The son has come and you've been left behind

The psychological trauma didn't lessen over the years. Instead, it continued to grow, as my fundamental beliefs added layer after layer of gripping fear, which my young developing brain had to somehow manage. My mental health could be summarized in two words: *precariously fragile*. Besides the obvious fear of Satan, fear of sinning, fear of sex, fear of growing up, fear of hell, fear of not measuring up, and fear of rejection and abandonment, there was yet another terror that seemed to trump the list: *the Rapture*. I'm not exaggerating when I claim my teenage years were spent nervously awaiting an impending thunderous trumpet blast from the heavens that would signify the end of the world. I don't mean to imply that I just sat around and waited for the end to come. I still attended school and church and enjoyed youth group activities. But no matter where I was or what I was doing, I knew Jesus could return at any moment. It was like turning the crank on the musical Jack-in-the-box to the tune of "Pop Goes the Weasel," "Dee-dee-dee-dee-diddly-ee-dee," and ever so carefully bracing myself for the sudden—wait for it . . . wait for it—*pop*! when Jesus would magically appear in the clouds to snatch all believers up in the air. Even as a Christian, this notion left me utterly paralyzed. Why in the world would Jesus not want to at least give us a heads-up? Couldn't he just whisper in the Christian's ear that he was going to come back in just a few minutes and not to be afraid? Maybe he could give us some preflight instructions to ease the jitters. The surprise element seemed cruel—almost sadistic. I couldn't understand why the congregation sang with such exuberance, "The

King is coming!" as if awaiting the arrival of Elvis in his glittery white pantsuit. I didn't like surprises, especially ones that involved being snatched up alive, like Dorothy and Toto in the tornado. But even worse than being taken in the rapture was the prospect of being left behind to face the Antichrist and possibly get my head lobbed off for not taking the "Mark of the Beast." *The Thief in the Night* series, viewed in nearly every charismatic church in America in the '70s and early '80s, painted a horrific picture of what it would be like to miss the rapture, and one thing I knew for sure, I wanted to be on that invisible spaceship with the rest of the saints.

My Christian zeal ramped up a few notches as I dedicated myself more and more to prayer, Bible study, and evangelism. Despite my best efforts, though, I had little assurance that I would be ready when Jesus made his surprise cameo appearance. My first encounter at Bible camp, along with rededications each year thereafter, provided some hope for me that my name was written in the Lamb's Book of Life. But when it came to the rapture, it didn't seem to matter if I was an "on fire" Christian. Even believers sin, and I wasn't perfect, so I worried that Jesus would come at a very inopportune moment, when I hadn't yet had a chance to repent for some unknown sin.

Consequently, every time I came home to an empty house, I panicked. If the clouds looked different, I panicked. If the roads were eerily empty, I panicked. If there is such a phobia called "fear of brass instruments," I think I had it, because even hearing a marching band in the distance would trigger a fight-or-flight response.

My sister-in-law took Jules and me to see *Bedknobs and Broomsticks*, our first movie in a theatre. As much as I wanted to enjoy the experience, I just sat white-knuckled and anxious, worrying that Jesus was going to come while I was hunkered down in this dark den of iniquity, indulging my senses with laughter and merriment. The only reason we had been allowed to go was my sister-in-law had convinced Mama that it was harmless and offered to pay for everything. I remember praying the whole time, under my breath, "Jesus, please don't come back yet! Please don't leave me behind." I reminded God, "It's Carolyn's fault that we are here!" Thankfully, when we left the theatre and headed toward the car, we could see no signs of the apocalypse, so I breathed a huge sigh of relief and silently thanked God that I had dodged that bullet.

One winter day, my sister and I were driving to the next town over to go sledding with the youth group. On the way, the CB radio broke the silence with a sudden, deafening blast of sound, in the same suspenseful and unexpected way the guy with the chainsaw jumps out from behind the bushes in a horror flick. Jules and I both let out the most blood-curdling shrill, not only because the noise had startled us but also because we had both automatically presumed it was the Rapture commencing! It took several minutes for our hearts to stop beating erratically and for our blood pressure to normalize. Of course, it's completely rational to mistake a CB radio blast for a warning from heaven that millions of people are about to vanish in the clouds, am I right? Someone? Anyone? No? We were clearly brainwashed to the point of paranoia, and of all the childhood traumas, I find this to be the most criminal. Sadly, the terror didn't end when I left my teens and entered adulthood. For at least thirty years, I have suffered from my own form of religiously induced PTSD. I startle awake in the middle of the night, somehow thinking the Rapture is happening, and I jump up, with my heart beating like a giant bass drum, disoriented and trembling, trying to pray and ready myself. The experience is utterly dreadful.

The unrelenting fear sent me clinging to Jesus, and I hoped others would find solace in His embrace as well. I was convinced that God had everything under control and whatever He had for me, if I believed in Him, was good. So I simply latched on to the delicious cherry-picked promises from the Bible that assured me of God's love, care, provision, power, and hope and credited the fear as a ploy from the "enemy" to make me anxious. I quoted the passage frequently, like a sacred mantra, "God has not given us a spirit of fear, but of power and love and a sound mind" (2 Timothy 1:7–8). Although the signs of the times were pointing to the reality that the end was near and calamity was about to befall the entire planet, I, nonetheless, would block out the unthinkable and joyfully sing and clap my hands with the rest of the congregation, our consolation anthem, "We win, we win, Hallelujah, we win! I read the back of the book and we win."

16

Jesus Freak in Neverland

My added passion for the Lord, prompted by Rapture-mania, manifested itself in peculiar ways, especially at the high school, a.k.a. my "harvest field," where I was commanded to fulfill the great commission. So what do you call a kid who wears Jesus paraphernalia to school, attends a weekly Bible study during lunch, stuffs gospel tracts in lockers and coat pockets, owns no secular albums, and has a Gideon New Testament peeking out of her backpack? Okay, besides *virgin*, take your pick: *weirdo, nerd, fruitcake, Jesus freak,* Joy Hoffmann, me. I was the clumsy misfit whom the jocks and cheerleaders mocked and patronized. Even Mr. Wallace, my social studies teacher, would roll his eyes in mild disgust when reading aloud my fake Coca-Cola button, "JESUS CHRIST, He's the real thing," or the sticker on my binder that said, "My God's not dead. Sorry about yours." I took to heart the message I had heard repeatedly at church, "If you're ashamed of God, *He* will be ashamed of you." Lord knows I didn't want the king of the universe claiming not to know me on Judgment Day, yet I couldn't help feeling my face get hot while performing my duty as a Christian mascot. I wanted to follow Christ *and* fit in, but I couldn't have both. When I considered what Jesus endured on the cross, it seemed the least I could do was suffer the momentary pain of isolation and social suicide at my tiny rural high school. Just like the day I refused to dance my way into the lunch line in sixth grade, I believed God was most pleased with me when I felt ostracized.

For my entire four years of high school, I lived in Never, Never Land. I *never* went on a date, *never* kissed a boy, *never* went to a party, *never* took a sip of alcohol, and *never* attended a rock concert or school dance. I didn't even go out for track, despite my PE teacher's encouragement, because there were occasional meets on Sunday, and Mama was convinced that running the one-hundred-yard dash would most certainly render the Sabbath unholy—a clear violation of the fourth commandment.

Let me back up a second. Okay. I did own one secular album, Simon and Garfunkel, but in my defense, I believed it was not only Christian but evangelistic as well. In "Mrs. Robinson," the lyrics clearly stated that Jesus loved her more than she would know and "Heaven holds a place for those who pray." Every time I heard the song, I got teary-eyed, thinking about how much poor dear Mrs. Robinson needed the Lord! I had no idea what the song was really about until I was in my thirties.

All these moments describing a typical American teen's rite of passage were off limits to me, and I lived in a parallel universe. I clung tightly to the one club that would fully embrace me: the church. In my sanctuary, I felt safe, cared for, and understood. Within the sacred walls, the God I loved and worshipped was revered instead of ridiculed, and the people on the outside who didn't believe were the foolish ones—not me. Inside the holy place, Jules and I were the poster kids every godly parent wished their teen would emulate. We were squeaky clean from head to toe, with excellent manners and servants' hearts, willing to help anywhere we were needed. The only trouble we ever got into during our entire teenage years, was when . . . umm . . . I'm so ashamed . . . okay, I'll just spit it out. We. Went roller skating. With the church youth group. Without permission. There I said it. Please don't hate me.

It was winter, our parents were touring the Holy Land, and I knew my brother wouldn't let us go, due to the blizzard. So I told him I had a piano lesson in Pocatello, which was true until my teacher called and cancelled at the last minute. But Ray didn't need to know that. Somehow I felt justified in my deception, since it was a church-sponsored event after all. This was our ticket to get a small taste of the wild side. By "wild" I mean going out on a school night. But as luck or, as my parents suggested, the Holy Spirit would have it, I backed into another car in the parking lot, denting my dad's pick-up truck. The other car was not damaged, as it was one of those old Cadillacs with the sharp, pointy-tail fins, that jabbed my dad's tailgate like a wieldy sword, while leaving no trace of its devastation on its own beastly frame. We were grounded for the entire month of December, and my dad decided not to fix the old GMC, so that every time we saw the crumpled artifact of our imprudence, we would remember what we had done—the gift of condemnation that just kept on giving! As Mama always warned, "Be sure your sins will find you out." And they did.

Besides this one unfortunate indiscretion, we were good girls. I even showed up early at the local nursing home to play the piano for the old folks before our main service on Sunday mornings, and we helped with children's church, doing puppets and skits. Jules and I also sang duets during the offertory, and I played piano solos on occasion. These things were not motivated by obligation or fear but, ironically, out of pure love for Jesus. This deity who humiliated, alienated, isolated, terrified, and threatened became the object of my unrelenting devotion. I wanted nothing more than to live my life completely and wholeheartedly consecrated to Christ and serving Him joyfully with my time and talents.

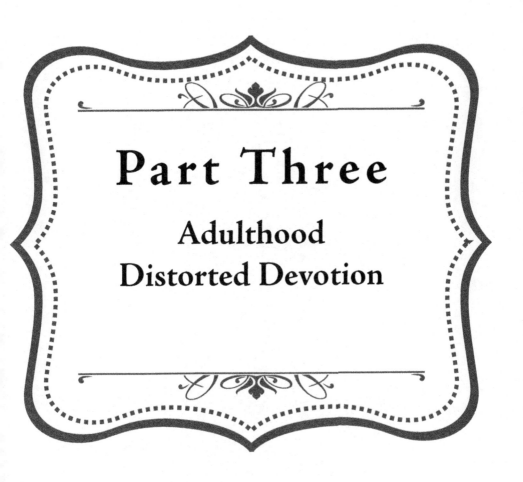

Part Three

Adulthood
Distorted Devotion

17

Trinity "Bridal" College

It was 1980, and Jesus was supposed to return to claim his spotless bride, the Church (the Pentecostals, that is, not the Baptists, Lutherans, Methodists, Presbyterians, Episcopalians, or Catholics). It was also the year Jules and I graduated from high school. I had desperately hoped that the celestial wedding would be delayed long enough for me to go to college, get married, and even have a kid or two, but the signs of the times were clearly pointing to my imminent exit into the clouds, sadly with my virginity still intact. In the spring, our high school auditorium had been converted to a college fair, where vendors from all the higher institutions of learning in the area set up booths to recruit students. Most of our classmates chose Idaho State University, the college only thirty minutes from home. The more daring ones went further north to the panhandle and landed at the University of Idaho in Moscow. The Mormon kids dutifully applied to Ricks College in Rexburg, or their mothership, BYU in Provo, Utah. A fair number of students joined the ROTC or enlisted in a branch of the armed forces. Then there was Jules and me. Our pre-Rapture holding pen wasn't even mentioned on a single brochure, let alone in a booth with zealous scouts, promising scholarships. Oh no. We chose a tiny, unaccredited, knock-off version of real college a thousand miles away in the town of Ellendale, North Dakota, population 1,200. The school was called Trinity Bible Institute, one of several colleges affiliated with the Assemblies of God, and with an enrollment of only 380 students. Of all the viable options at our disposal, why on earth would we choose *this* completely underwhelming place as our alma mater? We wanted to be equipped and ready to share the gospel, make disciples, and help usher in the second coming of Christ. And . . . our parents agreed to pay our entire tuition if we went there. I saw Trinity as a utopia of sorts, where Christianity along with strict accountability abounded. My fear of missing the Rapture fueled my desire to stay hemmed in with other like-minded folks. This school fit the bill. It was like military boot camp, only for believers, with a very stringent code of conduct. Girls could only wear dresses, despite the bitter North Dakota subzero temps in the winter. Boys had to wear button-down shirts and ties and dress slacks. Absolutely no PDA (public display of affection) was allowed. If a couple wanted to go on a date, they had to secure a chaperone to accompany them, the closest thing we ever had to a threesome.

Emergency sirens, typically used to alert the area of a tornado, signaled us, not into our underground bunkers but into our dorms for mandatory study hours from 6:00–9:00 p.m., no exceptions. Lights out at 10:00 p.m. was also strictly enforced. Many "past cur-few" nights were spent under the covers with a flashlight, preparing for a test, ready to quickly power off at the sound of the RA's footsteps in the hall, perhaps reminiscent of a young teen secretly devouring a forbidden *Playboy*, sans the gratification. If I was caught *studying* after hours—gasp! God forbid on a college campus—I would get a demerit, which went in my school file.

Our spiritual development was fostered through mandatory chapel services every morning where we spoke in tongues and lis-tened to an edifying sermon. Additionally, each student was required to sign up for a weekly time slot in the prayer room called the GAP, creating a twenty-four-hour prayer chain to intercede for the needs listed in a prayer request journal located in the room. This was a hot, stuffy, purple, ceiling-to-floor shag-carpeted cave with dim lighting and no windows. The second I went in to pray, I was overcome with drowsiness and found myself napping like a bear in hibernation. I felt guilty that the prayer chain had been repeatedly broken on my watch, but the physical conditions of the room made it impossible to stay awake. It may have been more exciting if the prayer requests had included juicy gossip or tantalizing dirt, but it was filled with stuff like arthritis, headaches, warts, goiter, etc., and no matter how spiritual I tried to be, praying for Mary's grandmother's hip replacement put me out faster than Nyquil p.m.

The rules of the school relaxed a bit when the ancient founding president died and a younger man came in to fill his fossilized footprints. The name changed from an institute to a college, for which I was grateful, because the original sounded a bit too much like an "institution" conjuring up images of crazy people in straitjackets, which was simply untrue—we did *not* have straightjackets. In our sophomore year, women could wear pants, only if they zipped in the back or side but not in the front (because only people with penises needed such an accommodation) and boys no longer were required to wear ties. By our junior year, everyone could wear blue jeans on the weekend but just not to class, and even those without a penis could finally wear front-zipped slacks. The chaperone mandate had also been lifted, and couples could, alas, venture out at their own risk without a third wheel accompanying them. Occasionally, though, a "weak" couple would slip up and be forced to confess in front of the *entire* student body during chapel that they had engaged in premarital sex. That was the moment one could hear a pin drop in the auditorium as all eyes fixed their gaze on the poor, embarrassed fornicators, who wished to God there was a magic trapdoor on the stage that would swallow them up and spit them out far, far away from the condemning stares. The consequence of academic probation or permanent expulsion held no sting compared to the shame of a public confession. If humiliation was the goal, though, I think my mama's solution would've been most effective. "I see you two like to have sex. Well why don't you just go ahead and start doing it right now in front of all these witnesses. Go ahead. Don't be shy. Come on. Get those legs up!" Not only would they have learned their lesson, but we would've also had one hell of a great chapel service! It was bad enough when students were found wanting, but one time, even a married staff member was caught in a sex scandal with a student. It wouldn't have been a laughing matter if not for the fact the offender's job title was Director of Student *Affairs.*

My college years were the absolute antithesis of what a typical college experience would be. Spring break consisted of forming a choir, visiting different churches in various cities, and sharing our testimonies about coming to faith in Jesus—a far cry from the "girls gone wild, Cancun, Spring Break edition" shown on HBO after hours. On the weekends, we would load up in a van and head to the city of Jamestown or Aberdeen and have our own version of a "good time," which included handing out gospel tracts to people on the street or going door to door to tell people about Jesus. I despised "witnessing" to strangers almost as much as the poor victims we preyed upon seemed to loathe us. Unsuspecting shoppers would be minding their own business, maybe enjoying a corn dog on a stick or an Orange Julius from the food court, when suddenly, they would find themselves trapped between the condiments and the napkin dispenser, being asked to repeat the "Sinner's Prayer." Going door to door was even worse because, invariably, the favored football team on TV would make a touchdown and the fans would go wild, while the poor victim, with Budweiser in hand, was kicking himself for answering the door. Now, besides missing the play of the century, he had to politely listen to the four freaking spiritual laws from nine-teen-year old Sister Mary and twenty-two-year-old Brother Robert, when all he really wanted was to get his fat ass back in that La-Z-Boy recliner. I still shudder when I think about it. And yet to admit I was embarrassed was to confess that I was ashamed of being a Christian and the very reason I feared God would "spit me out his mouth" for being only lukewarm and not on fire for Him.

When I completed my freshman year and Christ hadn't yet stormed through the clouds on his white stallion as predicted, I was hopeful that the calculations were far enough off, that I might have at least a few good years left on earth. Marriage and family were high on my bucket list, and I was convinced I would find my "godly" pastor/missionary husband before I graduated. "Trinity Bridal College," as we affectionately nicknamed it, was the '80s version of Christian Mingle or eHarmony for wannabe church leaders. Most of the girls

I knew were determined not to leave without their *Mrs.* degree, and I too was on a manhunt, looking for the perfect guy to partner with me in saving the world. His name was Troy.

18

A Match Made in Heaven

When introducing ourselves in front of a group, my favorite opener was, "Hi! My name is Joy, my husband's name is Troy, and my father's name is Roy." By then, everyone would be laughing, and Troy would pipe in, "And *my* father's name is . . . Frank!" It was a perfect icebreaker and one we used for many years. With rhyming names and similar passions for ministry, it seemed that our relationship was an obvious match made in heaven. We started at Trinity on the same day in 1980 and graduated together four years later. Troy was the only guy I ever kissed, and my virginity was the gift I gave him on our wedding day. By the Bible's standards, we had done everything right. We were a model couple, ordained by God to "go into all the world and make disciples," and we beautifully represented Trinity's alumni with our Christ-centered focus and vision for ministry. (If you need a minute to rinse the barf out of your mouth, I can wait.)

I had never officially dated. My trust issues from childhood remained imprinted on my psyche, making it difficult to see men as anything more than shallow, predatory sex fiends. I surmised that they were only attracted to women based on their looks, a standard with which I knew I couldn't compete. I hated jocks that objectified women and selfishly sifted lustfully through one relationship after another to satisfy their sexual fantasies. My self-esteem was too precarious to endure being rejected in this way, and so I gravitated toward the more gentle and effeminate guys, whom I deemed *safe*. I would bet my bottom dollar that my best friends in the music department were closeted gays, but coming out in the 1980s would've have been unthinkable, especially in a fundamentalist Bible College in the Midwest. This revelation comes in hindsight, as at the time, I was too naïve to recognize the signs. Even when one of them tragically died from AIDS a few years later in New York, I was still oblivious.

Troy wasn't overly effeminate, but he wasn't a jock either. He was the guy who still wore a suit and tie even after the dress code had relaxed and would *sign* the songs during worship, in our morning chapel services, not for the benefit of the deaf but just for his own personal edification, as a form of choreographed worship. The main thing that made him less threatening, besides his Napoleon Dynamite affinity for sign language, was the fact that he wasn't dating anyone. In fact, I had never seen him with a girl the entire two years we had been at school. As far as I knew, he hadn't broken any hearts, and I hoped he wouldn't break mine either. When we started hanging out together, everyone, including our professors, was rooting for us. Not only did our names rhyme but we even kind of looked alike, which was another confirmation, duly noted by the *spiritually* discerning. Troy met every criterion for being an eligible candidate for marriage, i.e. he loved Jesus and he had a penis, the latter detail taken on faith. So whatever red flags I noticed in terms of character were readily dismissed, as my God goggles had a special way of softening the rough edges. One day, for example, Troy needed a new pair of glasses and the optometrist in town gave him a free eye exam, knowing that he was a young college student with limited funds. In return for his generosity, it was expected that Troy would purchase his new glasses from the doctor, making it a win-win situation for both. But when it came to selecting the frames, Troy tactlessly informed the optometrist, "These are all ugly. I don't like any of them. Joy, let's go someplace that has decent frames." This was clearly an unmistakable breach of small-town etiquette. The man was visibly offended and gently said, "Troy, I just gave you a free exam. Are you sure you can't find a frame here that would work?" Troy responded, "I didn't ask you to do me any favors, and I'm under no obligation to buy your hideous glasses." He said *hideous*. I was horrified. Never in my life had I ever heard someone blatantly insult another person, especially an older gentleman who had just done him a favor, while showing absolutely no remorse. As he and I left, the kind man and I exchanged glances. I tried to convey my sympathy by mouthing the words, "I'm sorry," and he seemed to reciprocate the sentiments by nodding his head. I had told Mama about the incident and she warned, "The very way that he treats others is exactly how he will treat you once the honeymoon is over." I didn't believe her. She obviously didn't see what I could see. Troy was practically perfect. Sure, he had some jagged edges that needed polishing, but the important thing was that he was a believer with a penis, and that's all that truly mattered.

Our relationship was confusing at best, even from the beginning. I honestly never knew what his true feelings were because his passive-aggressive actions would constantly keep me guessing. For example, he would ask me out on some weekends but then routinely ignore me in the school cafeteria at dinner. Sometimes he would sit with me in chapel, and other times, he would walk past without so much as a hello. We held hands occasionally and even kissed a couple of times, but that was the extent of our "physical" relationship. Like me, I knew he wanted to remain sexually pure, and so I attributed his prudish restraint as a sign of his commitment to obeying Jesus. If our relationship could be personified, it was "Pat," the androgynous character Julia Sweeney played on *Saturday Night Live*. The tip of the iceberg was when he came home with me at Christmas to meet my family but then ignored me the whole time he was there, refusing even to sit next to me on the couch. I felt like a fool in front of my nieces, nephews, parents, and siblings, who were expecting at least a nominal public display of affection since he was after all, "my boyfriend." On the road trip back to college, I decided I just needed to know where we stood because the constant mixed messages were making me crazy. I asked, "What do you think of me? Are we just friends or are we dating? Do you like me? Do you love me? Do you have feelings for me? Please just help me understand, because I can't figure you out." His immediate reaction was anger that I had the gall to ask him to clarify the relationship. I mean, how dare I challenge his obtuse communication skills? He responded by putting two words together that no girl seeking reassurance wants to hear in the same sentence. He sarcastically claimed he loved me all right—about as much as a nagging mother! At least he didn't use *hideous*. Still, he insinuated there was something inherently wrong with *me* to vocalize concern or to express my feelings. Humiliated, I began piecing together the rules of the relationship: Don't share your feelings. Don't ask him about his feelings. Keep playing the guessing game regarding expectations, and don't ask for clarification. Most importantly, don't seek an apology or he will break up with you. Sadly, I learned this the hard way when I asked him to retract his hurtful "nagging mother" comment. When we arrived back at campus, we went our separate ways, marking the end of my pathetically short-lived dating career.

But I couldn't get over him. I truly believed we were still "meant" to be together, despite the evidence to the contrary. Religious superstition has a way of skewing reality, and I was still latching onto the notion that our rhyming names had something to do with our destiny! I'm not even joking! On a deeper level, I knew I wanted to be married and my prospects were slim. To have gone through four years of high school and now four years of college without any serious suitors—correction: without *any* suitors—I didn't want to let go of the one chance, though imperfect, that I had. I was sure that if I made no demands of Troy and if I simply loved and served him and fed his ego, asking nothing in return, he could love me and discover the loyal gift that I would be to him. Despite my prayers and wishful thinking, I didn't see any immediate signs that we were going to get back together, even though he didn't date anyone else while we were broken up, nor did I. Still, my plan to get my degree and ride off into the sunset with my new husband needed to be adjusted. I decided after graduation, I would pick up some extra music and art classes at Evangel College, a larger school, also affiliated with the Assemblies of God, located in Springfield, Missouri. Providentially, Troy too made plans to move to Springfield to attend the Assemblies of God Theological Seminary. What were the odds? Of course, I interpreted this news as a crystal-clear beacon from heaven! In my mind, the clouds had parted and the cherubim and seraphim were belting out their angelic symphony: "Together forever! Hallelujah, hallelujah, ha-le-e-lu-u-jah!" The clues seemed to scream of our pre-ordained union, yet somehow, Troy wasn't paying attention and was, in fact, downright oblivious to the angelic love ballad. Perhaps some good old-fashioned manipulation in the name of Jesus was in order. With mutual friends and teachers telling him what a "perfect" couple we would be and reminding him that he *needed* to find a wife, Troy succumbed to the peer pressure and decided to give "us" another shot. Of course, my rose-colored glasses sanitized the entire ordeal by erasing all traces of coercion and "behind the scenes" plotting so I could proclaim to the world how we "miraculously" got back together at the end of our senior year and how, before classes started up in Missouri, in the fall, he got down on one knee and asked me to be his wife. "Hallelujah, hallelujah, ha-le-e-lu-u-jah."

19

Give Me a Sign

There was only one thing that could possibly trump my excitement of getting married. And it happened on Thanksgiving weekend, one month before the big day. My parents had come to Springfield to visit and to help me pick out my dress. Troy and I were sitting in their hotel room, when Mom—no longer "Mama" now that I was an adult—hinted that she had a secret. But she wasn't about to let it out all at once. This was gossip so juicy and delicious it had to be savored. She threw out the first bait. "By the way, Joy, someone is looking for you."

I had no idea what she was talking about. Puzzled, I asked, "What do you mean? Who could possibly be looking for me?"

Mom smiled mischievously, knowing she had me hooked. She pulled out a small classified ad, clipped from the *Bannock County News*, and waved it like a flag, before slowly handing it over to me for a closer look. As I began to read, my heart started to race. I couldn't believe what I was reading!

> Brother seeking information concerning twin sisters, Joy and Julie. Family separated in 1965. Please call Steve collect.

After all this time, I'm still at a loss for words to fully express the shock and awe of that moment. I was absolutely convinced, beyond a doubt, that God had orchestrated this event, and I was undone.

Fuck the million other things I had prayed for but didn't get. None of it mattered now because I finally got my first true, legit miracle. My entire life, I had wondered what had ever become of my family, and for the first time, I had a chance to find out. When Jules and I were in high school, we managed a brief encounter with Dean while attending a music festival at Pocatello High. Apparently, shortly after joining the Hoffmanns, while passing by the school, we pointed to a barbershop across the street and exclaimed, "That's where old Daddy works." Time has a way of erasing memories, though, and this piece of information became lost to us until Mama had reminded us, many years later, while driving by the very spot. When we arrived at the school and saw the red, white, and blue swirling pole with "Dean's Barber" on the sign, we seized the opportunity to satisfy our curiosity. Getting Curtis, one of our friends, to come with us and join in our ruse, we went into the shop to simply ask, "How much for a haircut?" Dean, touting a long white beard and a sun visor, pointed to a weathered tagboard sign, probably posted from the time his shop opened, and said, "Well, a haircut is $3 just like the sign there says, and $2.25 for those over sixty." There was a long pause. We stared as inconspicuously as we could, trying to memorize his aging features and have something to take with us to add to, confirm, or revise our chapter 1. He seemed quiet and friendly and very ordinary, like someone's sweet old grandpa, completely unlike the drunk, angry monster we had always envisioned. As we studied his face and he studied ours, I wondered if there had been any recognition. I clearly had inherited his nose and chin but was too giddy to hold it against him at that moment. I wanted to blurt out, "Hi, Dad! Surprise!" but I refrained, accepting the likely possibility that he might not be prepared for a spontaneous family reunion. We thanked him for the information, said good-bye, wishing him a good day, and headed back to the school, full of titillating glee that we had just met our birth father.

That was the closest encounter I believed I would ever have with my family of origin and resigned myself to not ever being reunited. But now, an invitation was literally at my fingertips. My brother Steve was looking for me. This meant that he remembered his twin sisters and wanted to know what had happened to them. The constant nagging questions, "Would they remember us and would they want to see us?" was answered by this tiny 2" × 2" classified ad. The answer was yes, and I was ecstatic.

The phone number was staring me in the face, but I was paralyzed. My big brother was a stranger, and I suddenly felt nervous. Instead of calling the number on the ad, I dialed Jules and asked her to make the first contact. About thirty minutes later, the phone rang. When I picked up, I heard the voice of Steve, who said, "Hello, sis! I just got off the phone with Jules!" Then his voice broke as he tried to convey the depth of gratitude he felt to finally be talking with his baby sisters. He shared with me that finding us had been his lifelong ambition. He had gone through the court system, but the adoption records had been sealed. As a last-ditch effort, he placed an ad in the town newspaper where we had been born, hoping we had been adopted nearby and someone would have information about us. He asked when we could meet in person. I told him I was getting married the next month, in Pocatello, and he was overjoyed. He promised to come to Idaho, from his home in Reno, so we could have our first face-to-face reunion. After we hung up, I couldn't stop smiling. The phone rang again. This time, it was my oldest brother, Matt. "Hey, Joy! Steve told me he found you! Do you know how long I've waited for this day? Twenty years, to be exact!" He proceeded to tell me story after story of our childhood—how I loved to wear cowboy boots, but they were always on the wrong feet. And how my glasses were attached to my ears with rubber bands and I looked like Tweety Bird. He shared with me how he and Steve would steal outfits from neighboring clotheslines for us and go door to door asking for food when there was nothing in the house for us to eat. At thirteen, he had been our caregiver and did his best to protect us and take care of us when Dean was drinking. "One day," he explained, "two cars pulled up to the house. Chris was placed in one car, and Jules and you were placed in the other, while Steve and I had been sent on an errand. When we got home, you were gone! Just like that. No good-byes. Nothing. The social workers came for us too, promising to take us where you were, but they lied." Matt started crying, emotions still raw as he began to relive the devastation of that moment.

After Matt and I hung up, I was starting to feel emotionally drained as the impact of it all was sinking in. My tiny, fragmented, disjointed memories of my life before the Hoffmanns were suddenly expanding and exploding. The missing pages were being filled in, and I was beginning to get a sense of who I was and how I fit into the Slater clan.

The phone rang one more time. Chris, who was fifteen months older than Jules and me, echoed the joyful sentiments of Matt and Steve. "I was reunited with the boys only two years ago," he said, "through the LDS church. We couldn't wait to find you girls!" Chris had been in a foster home for a couple of years after leaving the Slaters but then was put back in the system when his foster parents adopted a special needs child instead of him. He ended up being cared for temporarily by an elderly couple from the relief society at the Mormon Church, who had already raised their kids. But whenever the social worker would come to visit, he would hide because he didn't want to go to yet another family. One day, when he disappeared at the social worker's arrival, his foster parents finally said with resignation, "Ah, what the heck. We'll keep him," as if he were a cute little stray puppy showing up on their doorstep.

I couldn't wait to sit down and talk in depth with each of my brothers and to hear their story from the very beginning. We planned to meet during the Christmas break in Pocatello sometime before my wedding day on New Year's Eve, and Matt, Steve, Chris, Jules, and I would be together for the first time in twenty years.

If I had any doubts that God was real and that he could perform miracles, they vanished that night because I was convinced that this encounter was divinely orchestrated. I thought, *What are the chances that I would get to meet my birth family just before getting married?* God knew I needed closure before I could embark on this next "new beginning" of sorts. I concluded that this *had* to be a miracle performed solely for my benefit. I saw this as confirmation that I was supposed to marry Troy and that I was in God's perfect will. Any doubts or insecurities became blurred as a bright and promising future came into focus. If this was God's doing, then nothing could stand in our way of marital bliss.

20

Chapter One Addendum

Word spread like wildfire at Evangel College that I had just been reunited with my long-lost brothers, and my story made it on the front page of the school paper. My special wedding day had been upstaged by the Slater family reunion, and between these two earth shattering events, I could hardly focus on my studies. Several days after my whirlwind Thanksgiving to remember, I received yet another call, this time in my dorm room. The woman on the other end identified herself as Lillie, my birth mom. My mother. Oh my god! My heart started to race. The phantom person I had heard about in name only but had no memories to make her real, the woman described by one solitary, unflattering adjective, thanks to the eye doctor—*my mother*—was on the line. There she was, introducing herself while the seismic activity in my gut was reaching a catastrophic magnitude. I was about to erupt—not in anger or sadness but from pure, unrelenting happiness. I was in awe that God had reunited me with not only my brothers but also this elusive woman, who had conceived and given birth to me. I couldn't sit still. I paced around my quarters like a first-time father in the waiting room, anticipating the delivery of his offspring. She shared her story of desperately trying to care for us but being unable to because of Dean's alcoholism.

"All the money went to his addiction and nothing was left for the children," Lillie explained. "Then I met Carl, fell in love, and together, we moved to Reno, Nevada, to start over. I brought you and Jules with me and tried my best to take care of you. I really did."

Her voice resonated regret. She continued, "One day, though, I came home from work to find the sitter gone and the two of you alone in the house unattended. I tried not to think about what could've happened to you. I started to take you to the restaurant with me while I waited tables, but I knew that sitting in a booth all day was no life for toddlers. So I sent you back to live with Dean just until I could get on my feet financially."

"Is that when we were put in foster care?" I asked.

"Yes. Your dad got arrested on a DUI, and all of you were placed in emergency foster care until he got out. Then he got another DUI, and this time you were taken for good. I tried to get you back, but the social workers said you were better off where you were and not to fight it."

Lillie started to cry. "It was the hardest thing to give you up, but you kids never stopped being my children and I never stopped loving you."

My God goggles had dulled the pain over the years and nearly erased the lingering questions from my past, yet there were some hurts that were too deep to be altered by color, light, and a different perspective. They remained safely buried in my soul and didn't come to the surface until that moment. I realized that all along, I had felt unworthy of being loved by my birth parents, which fed and nurtured the insecurities with my adoptive family. In that moment, I saw a glimpse of that homely little girl with fresh eyes. Maybe there was something endearing about her after all. Lillie humbly asked if she could join the family reunion in Idaho. I didn't hesitate even for a second with my resounding "yes!" I longed to see her, hug her, and compare genetic similarities. It was too good to be true. Not only would I get to see my brothers face to face, but I would also get to meet the woman who carried me in her womb and in her heart for the past twenty-three years. I felt whole and complete. I knew who I was. My Chapter 1 was written.

21

Family Reunion

December 31, 1984, will forever top the list of my most memorable and life-changing days as I met my birth family, got married, *and* lost my virginity—all in one fell swoop! We met at Elmer's Pancake and Steakhouse, a restaurant only a block away from the church. We started attending the First Assembly of God in Pocatello when Jules and I were in sixth grade and spent many, many Sunday nights at Elmer's, eating boysenberry cobbler after the evening service with church friends. We knew the place well, but even with the familiarity, the butterflies in my stomach were going crazy. I couldn't pinpoint any one emotion. My brain and heart were experimental chefs mixing together a crazy new concoction comprised of fear, joy, curiosity, anticipation, wonder, happiness, and suspense, along with other diarrhea-inducing ingredients. My brother Matt met Jules and me outside, hugging us with a magnitude that matched his deep and heartfelt sentiments. Our mutual elation was apparent as we all valiantly fought to hold back the tears. He escorted us in and led us to the back room, where the rest of the family was already seated and waiting. And just like Van Gogh unveiling his *Starry Night* masterpiece, the doors opened and the elusive Slater family was finally revealed. The tables were shaped in a *T*, and at the head sat a man and a woman, the matriarch and patriarch of this broken and scattered family, Dean and Lillie. Though they had been divorced for two decades, there they sat, representing a marriage that once was and the offspring that came from their union. I couldn't help but grin, seeing Dean and remembering our covert mission in the barbershop five years prior. I had no idea he would be present, but my senses were already experiencing such stimulus overload that I hardly had a chance to be properly surprised. I was eager to ask if he had remembered our chance encounter, but of course he hadn't. He expressed to us his overwhelming regret that he had lost everything due to his thirty-year love affair with alcohol and that he had finally gotten help through AA and had been completely sober for a whole year. Lillie looked nervous and reserved, wondering if she would find acceptance from her long-lost daughters. But I knew I loved her the second our eyes met. I assured her that Jules and I had been raised well by a very loving family and that she did the right thing to allow us a chance at a better life. Her features softened, and she became more relaxed. I slowly began to see her true self emerge—a sweet, smart, funny woman with a very tender and compassionate heart. And suddenly, I realized my Chapter 1 would need revising yet again. Lillie had soft, plump, inviting "motherly" features, perfect for comforting and coddling a crying baby, but she certainly wasn't, by my estimate, obese. All the years of worry, agonizing about my weight and starving myself because of my genetic predisposition, based on a tiny shred of information that may have been true at one time, was now completely irrelevant.

Matt was the most animated in the group and he talked nonstop, just wanting to catch us up on everything we had missed over the past twenty years. He had a box of pictures that he had salvaged when the family split apart and took it upon himself, as the oldest, to be the historian. Picture after picture was pulled from the box and passed around. It was first-grade "show and tell" all over again. "This is your Uncle Ben, who lives in Canada. He was the one we were going to stay with before you got taken away. And here is your grandma, who lived with us for a while and helped take care of you. Joy, you always looked just like her!" My poor brain couldn't keep track of all the names and faces, but with each image, I was gaining a sense of my larger extended family, people I would never meet, except vicariously through Matt's photos and descriptions. The most prized possessions in the box, however, were the baby pictures of Jules and me. Our earliest portraits started at age three when we joined the Hoffmanns, and in some ways, it felt as though we had never been babies. My heart melted to see Jules and I together with our little bald heads—me with a fussy little expression and Jules with her sweet angelic look of innocence and contentment. Another treasure that captured my heart was a black-and-white snapshot of the five children together. The boys were sitting on the hood of a car, shirtless, with cut-off blue jeans and army-buzzed heads, while Jules and I, with tangled, messy hair, stood in front, also shirtless and in our underwear. While I couldn't remember the moment when the picture was taken, it, nonetheless, felt familiar. My brothers had been frozen in time—stuck at the age I last remembered them, and the picture brought clarity to the vague images I carried with me over the years.

As a devout believer, I couldn't help but wonder if any of my family was "saved." I was devastated to hear that Chris had been adopted into a Mormon family and had only recently returned from his two-year mission in Southern California. Others seemed to have their ties in the Mormon Church as well but didn't regularly attend church. The Mormons were some of our (Pentecostals) biggest opponents in evangelism. We were convinced that they were most certainly destined for Hell, and so we were in a race to save the "lost" quickly before the Latter-Day Saints got to them and ruined their chances of making it to heaven. Mom mocked them by saying LDS stood for ladies' dirty stockings (because of their holy underwear that they weren't allowed to remove), and much was made about their belief in baptism for the dead and multiple levels of heaven where saints would rule their own planet. I saw Jules and I as the lucky ones, blessed by God to be adopted into a Pentecostal family where we were taught the "right" things about God and the plan of salvation. We had a corner on "truth," and we knew that everyone else, even other Christian churches, had it wrong. I wrestled with the idea that God had chosen Jules and me to respond to the gospel but He allowed Chris to be adopted and brainwashed into a "cult." And poor Matt and Steve got no spiritual direction at all, as Dean never stepped foot in church. With the realization that I could've been just like them, spiritually *dead* but for the grace of God, I felt a surge of superiority that God had seen something in Jules and me that had warranted our rescue. Amidst the love, warmth, tears, and joyful reconnecting, my mind switched the scene from family reunion to mission field. I looked around the room and saw not only loved ones but lost souls. It was Jules's and my *duty* to evangelize these "sinners." So beyond the emotional comfort and closure I felt, I believed the primary purpose of our reunion was a spiritual one. I was convinced God wanted to use my Christian wedding to witness to the Slaters. Remember Joseph being kidnapped and sold into slavery to save his family later? I believed this was my fate. The pain, dysfunction, separation, and loss were merely a part of God's plan all along! Had our family not been obliterated, I wouldn't have become a Christian. If I hadn't been saved, how could my family hear the good news? This tragedy of epic proportions, as seen through the lens of faith, transformed itself, instead, into a magical story of hope and grace.

22

Torn between Two Mothers

As the reunion was dying down, Lillie confessed, "I know I said I wouldn't come to the wedding because I don't want to step on any toes, but I've missed every milestone for the past twenty years in your life. It would make me so happy and proud to see you get married."

I had created a musical slide show of Troy's and my childhood to be shown at the end of the ceremony. Lillie would get to see her twins riding trikes, smiling with missing teeth, posing as awkward teenagers and graduating from college. And most importantly, she would hear the "Good News" woven through every song, prayer, and sermon. It was no accident that Lillie was now asking permission to attend. God was at work! So Troy, Jules, and I agreed that it would probably be just fine that she inconspicuously attend since it would be a rather large gathering and she and Dean could likely slip in unnoticed. And if Mom found out, surely she would understand how important it was to allow Lillie this one special request, since it was, after all, God's will.

Within five minutes of Dean and Lillie entering the foyer, the gossip spread like wildfire, and the blaze could not be contained until every last person knew that Joy and Jules's birth parents had shown up. I tried to block out any potential negative backlash and just enjoy my big day. For me, the moment was perfect. I had my birth parents and my adoptive parents, along with my biological brothers and my adoptive brothers and of course, my twin, whom I loved dearly, all at *my* wedding, celebrating with *me*. I couldn't have asked for anything more.

When the ceremony was over and the slide show began, I could see my brothers crying. Lillie was clearly touched as well, dabbing her eyes with a tissue as my childhood flashed across the screen in five-second intervals. When we met in the fellowship hall for the reception, the Slaters and Hoffmanns met for the first time, face to face. I remember them stoically shaking hands. Never in my wildest dreams would I have envisioned the merging of my two worlds on the day I would ride off into the sunset with my prince, and yet it was happening before my eyes. It was obvious that the exchange of niceties was forced and uncomfortable for both sets of parents, but I was so proud that an effort was being made. And as I paused to soak it all in, I couldn't help but thank God for making such a day possible. It was the perfect start to my new life as Mrs. Joy Corbin.

23

Leaving and Cleaving

The next day, however, I felt like Cinderella after being stripped of the magic pumpkin carriage, horses, gown, and slippers. All the fairy dust of the night before was gone, and Troy and I were packed and ready to drive off together as husband and wife in our Buick Skylark we had been given as a gift from my parents. But when we pulled up to my house to say good-bye and thank Mom and Dad for the beautiful wedding and for being so gracious with Dean and Lillie, I got the cold shoulder. Mom would have nothing to do with me. She wouldn't speak to me or hug me or wish me well. She turned and walked away when I tried to approach her. I didn't know what to do. My full, happy, optimistic heart was crumbling into a thousand tiny pieces. I couldn't bear to have Mom not kiss me and send me off with her blessing. I was moving two thousand miles away, and I needed to hear her say she loved me. I needed to tell her the same. I needed the closure of "goodbye." But she refused, leaving me to carry the heaping weight of guilt on my shoulders. When I could see that my efforts were useless, Troy and I slowly stepped out the door in stunned silence and headed toward the car as I burst into uncontrollable sobbing. Jules followed us out and explained why Mom was so hurt, but of course, we already knew. This was supposed to be about the Hoffmanns and the marriage of their daughter, but instead, it became more about Joy and Jules's birth parents showing up. I had gotten so caught up in the emotion of seeing my birth family and wanting to evangelize them that I naively assumed Roy and Jeannie would understand the big picture. After all, if this whole thing was the Holy Spirit's doing, I had assumed Mom would surely be on board. We pulled out of the driveway and off to our honeymoon, my joy overshadowed by brokenness, while Jules returned to the house and attempted to do damage control.

This story, like so many others, accentuated the belief that my sanctification process necessarily entailed some form of rejection or humiliation. Unless I was constantly identifying with Christ's sacrifice, I couldn't grow as a Christian. So even on the happiest occasion of my life, down deep, I expected God to sabotage it in some way, and He did.

As I donned my rose-colored glasses in search of a palatable explanation, a less painful, sugarcoated alternative presented itself. "Perhaps this was the Lord's way of helping me to leave and cleave," I concluded. I had heard sermons about girls who would run home to "Mommy" whenever they got in a fight with their husband. Maybe God was just cutting the apron strings for my own sake. If that was the case, I had no right to feel hurt. God was doing this for my good. Suppressing the pain, I thanked Jesus for helping me to wean myself from Mom's approval so that I could become "one flesh" with my husband. I had peace that God was working everything out for his glory, as he had promised.

24

The Honeymoon from Hell

Our honeymoon was awful. All my sexual thoughts, desires, and fantasies that had been bottled up so tightly since puberty continued to retain their shape of captivity even after the lock box had been removed and my inhibitions had been set free. I was nervous and self-conscious about my body and about as rigid as an ironing board, partly because I had yet to hear that I was beautiful or sexy by any man, let alone my new husband. And like a budding flower, I couldn't just open up and blossom without first being swaddled in warm sunlight and doused with gentle rain. But nurturing wasn't one of Troy's selling points, and his attempt at "watering" my garden often felt like a high-compression gardening hose in the face. Just to be clear, this is not a graphic *blowjob* reference but merely a metaphor to describe my feelings. Anyway, point being, grace and tact were traits he would have to develop over time. Moreover, months before, when I had asked Troy if he was excited about having sex, he said, "No, not really." From the stories my friends told, I knew this was not a typical guy response. I concluded that he was either just suppressing his desire since we weren't married yet or that he didn't find me appealing enough to be tempted. My fears were relieved when we had secretly "made out" in the days leading up to the wedding. The sparks were flying as his hands made their way up my blouse, and it was obvious we were both physically aroused. So I convinced myself that he was merely trying to please God by feigning a disinterest in physical pleasure, and yet the possibility of the latter still left me feeling insecure as we ventured through this once forbidden but now encouraged frontier.

We drove across country back to Missouri and then flew to Florida, where we boarded a cruise ship headed to the Bahamas. On day three of the road trip, I tried to shake off some of my fuddy-duddy reticence by inviting him to take a bath with me, something I had heard other newlyweds enjoyed. I imagined lots of bubbles, giggling, kissing, playful splashing, and imaginary hearts floating above our heads as we gazed into each other's eyes. Nervously, for the first time, I undressed in front of him with the bright bathroom light glaring harshly down on my nakedness, making me feel completely vulnerable and exposed. Troy's reaction was one of complete disinterest as he made no discernable gesture whatsoever that he liked what he saw. I felt like a deer in the headlights, as I frantically searched for clues of lust or fire in his eyes or a faint smile on his face denoting pleasure. But all I could read from his body language was apathy, which I translated into rejection. Suddenly I was reliving one of my recurring nightmares of being at school and realizing, with shock and unthinkable horror, that I had somehow forgotten my pants. The notion that sitting in the bathtub together making bubble beards would be romantic was terribly overrated. It felt more like a TSA security inspection at the airport. After a few minutes of painful awkwardness, I slipped on my robe, covering my embarrassment, and made a note to self, "Don't try that again. He's not attracted to your body." By day four, in our hotel room, Troy was already "not in the mood" and simply gave me a peck on the cheek, as he rolled on his side with his back toward me. Was it because he had seen me naked in the light and was having buyer's remorse? I had always been self-conscious about my body, painfully aware that my dimensions didn't seem to match the flawless standard of beauty portrayed in the media. Nonetheless, I still had enough sense to know that this wasn't normal. We were on our honeymoon and should've been "making whoopee" day and night, for God's sake, and yet there we lay, two old, tired twenty-three-year-olds, bored and disillusioned after only four days post-virginity. I quietly asked him if everything was okay. He grunted a pathetic and unconvincing "Yeah, I guess." When asked, what was wrong and why he didn't want to have sex, he said, with disgust, "Well, I don't particularly enjoy making love to a limp, wet dishrag!" I thought the "nagging mother" comment was hurtful, but this time, he had outdone himself. I was utterly devastated. I still feel the sting of his unkind rebuke thirty years later as I write this. Any confidence that I had was crushed by his cruel insensitivity. I wanted to please him, to satisfy him, but I was already written off as a failure before I could even learn what to do. And to be fair, I didn't understand what part my submissive role in the relationship played with regards to sex. This couldn't be as bad as it seemed, could it? *No, of course not*, I rationalized. *Everyone's honeymoon starts off awkward. I mean, what husband hasn't compared his wife to a soggy towel at one time or another?* I didn't know any personally, but I was sure I wasn't alone. Further, I had to remind myself that I hadn't exactly had an opportunity to practice, what with being a virgin and all. The unworthy voice, I constantly tried to suppress, whispered her spiteful accusation. "You don't deserve to be treated with kindness and respect. You are ugly and unlovable." There was no alternate voice or personal experience to suggest otherwise. I had only my faith reminding me of my depravity apart from Christ. I was nothing, and I deserved nothing. The rejection I felt did not propel me to seek happiness for myself but rather to try harder to please Troy. In my mind, he had gotten a raw deal by marrying me because I wasn't pretty enough or sexy enough to meet his needs. And yet, strangely, I was still absolutely convinced that God had brought us together. I recounted the signs and wonders we had witnessed confirming that our union was stamped and sealed with God's approval. We were meant to be together. I was sure of it. We had to be! Our names were Troy and Joy! We rhymed, goddamn it.

25

Keep Hands, Feet, and Objects to Yourself

I eventually learned that it would take more than matching "diph-thongs" (*oy*) to make a marriage work. As hopeful as I was that we would get the intimacy piece worked out, we certainly weren't making very big strides. Trying to rid myself of the humiliating "limp dishrag" label, I made a gallant effort to be playful. Admittedly, I probably hadn't yet mastered the crafty art of seduction, but still, it felt like chunks of my heart were eroding away each time I would don my sexy lingerie to entice him, only to be treated like an annoying fly buzzing around his pizza. Even when we would just lie in bed together, if my foot so much as brushed against his leg, he would sigh heavily and tell me to stay on my own side, reminiscent of siblings forced to share a bed while the cousins were visiting. If my body accidentally bumped into him more than once, he would stomp out of bed, grab his pillow, and sleep elsewhere. Even during the day, he wouldn't allow me to sit next to him on the couch or try to snuggle. He would simply get up and move to another chair, leaving me to feel as though the fourth grade "cooties" we passed around as kids were actually a thing, and I, unfortunately, had them. As hurtful as it was for him to constantly push me away, it soon became my new "norm," and I grew to anticipate the safe distance I was to remain from him.

One day, after church as we were entering through the automatic doors of the grocery store I felt his hand on my back. I remember it so vividly because at first it startled me, and I jumped. But then it was like an electric shock of warmth shooting through my body. He had invaded his own space bubble to touch me in public, and it felt wonderful. I momentarily realized how starved I was for simple, basic human connection. Unfortunately, what I perceived as an attempt at affection was really a push, as he was moving me out of the way so a shopper could retrieve a cart. I know it sounds ridiculous, but that meaningless four-second encounter exposed a nerve so raw that I couldn't stop the tears as my emotional dam burst. Pushing the cart through the produce department, I held my breath, trying to regain control before Troy could witness my meltdown and wonder what the hell I could possibly be crying about. In that moment, I realized the only person allowed to meet my physical, emotional, and sexual needs was Troy, and he was using his power as leverage to punish me for his own unhappiness. There was no amount of leopard-print negligees or bottled pheromones that could fan the flame of desire. What he seemed to loathe the most was the "me" that couldn't be altered or enhanced. He didn't like *me*. Everything about our relationship whispered this harsh truth, but it didn't fit with what we believed about God sovereignly and miraculously joining couples like us together. Certainly, God hadn't made a mistake, but was it possible that that we had just misread the clues? Either way, it didn't matter. We had made a solemn vow in the presence of witnesses that we would stay married, for better or for worse, until death do us part. Love or no love, we were stuck together. And being a person who seeks approval by pleasing others, I couldn't give up and declare defeat. I was going to make it my life ambition to gain his love, not only for his sake but for mine as well. I would try to be the best wife he could ever ask for, and with God's help, I would make him happy or die trying.

Although on the surface, our relationship looked doomed, my reservoir of optimism painted a different picture. I could see my own unhappiness as an opportunity to repent of selfishness and to give myself fully to my husband's needs and desires, a promising example of *seeing the glass half full*. The ongoing message that played constantly in my thoughts was that following Jesus was costly. And the more I suffered, the more like Christ I would become. So I considered it pure "joy" to be rejected, knowing God was shaping my character and making me fit for heaven. I was excited and hopeful that one day we would have an amazing story to share of God's grace. I clung to the verses that promised joy in the wake of sorrow and growth, in the midst of pain. After all, marriage wasn't about my personal happiness; Eve was created for Adam's pleasure and not the other way around. Remembering the lessons learned from childhood about pleasing God through self-denial, I believed the ache deep in my soul was confirmation that I was, indeed, in the center of God's perfect will.

26

Submission 101

It doesn't take long to hit rock bottom when one's highest pinnacle is not a mountaintop, but rather a stepladder. Still we teetered on the bottom rung for several months until we finally hit the ground with a dull, throbbing thud. The pastoral counselor gave us little hope, pronouncing our marriage practically dead on arrival and explaining that if our relationship was to be resuscitated, it needed a radical overhaul. The remedy? Bible studies. Homework assignments. Accountability. Troy, instead, had a different idea. "Let's run away," he suggested. So we did. We loaded up our possessions, left my car at Aunt Ruby and Uncle Bill's farm to be picked up by my parents after we had found a place to settle, and started driving. We had only enough money for gas and $10 per week for food, which consisted of a loaf of bread, a jar of peanut butter, and ramen noodles that we tried cooking with an electric tea pot, in the only places where we could find an outlet—public restrooms. Our tent was our home for the next four months as we wandered across the country looking at potential seminaries for Troy to attend and occasionally trading our campsite for the basement sofa bed of several Trinity alumni with whom we had kept in touch. Lest one gets any warm, fuzzy romantic notions about two young newlyweds hitting the open road without a destination, living in a canvas dome, and cooking noodles in shit-scented rest stops, let me go ahead and burst that bubble right now.

One day, as we were driving, Troy turned on the radio to listen to music. My speaker was blocked on my side from the all the stuff we were hauling, so I innocently turned up the dial a notch. Troy immediately turned it down. "I can't hear it on my side," I told him. "I need to turn it up just a smidge." The second my fingers touched the dial, his fingers were right there to counter my move. Before I could even blink or formulate a token "What the heck?" out of nowhere, I felt an unexpected sting as he backhanded me across my face. With angry veins bulging from his temples and his index finger pointed at me like a loaded revolver, he began to slowly speak with a deliberate pause between each word, for emphasis. "Don't—you—ever—touch the dial—again! Do—you—understand?" During our first few months of marriage, he had physically grabbed me and aggressively shoved me onto the couch while getting within an inch of my face screaming at me when I expressed that I was feeling inse-cure (as if *that* would make me feel better), but he hadn't yet actually hit me. I was stunned. Here we were heading down the highway in the middle of nowhere, with absolutely no support and no backup plan, and I was sitting next to a man who thought it was perfectly fine to smack me in the face for adjusting the radio volume. I enter-tained the idea of jumping out of the car at the next stop, but whom would I call and where would I go? In my helplessness, I started to pray. The answer seemed to always be within reach. All my years in church and Bible College, being groomed for biblical womanhood, I knew the solution before even seeking counsel from the Holy Spirit. I just needed to be submissive. If my husband said not to touch the radio dial, my wifely obligation was to obey. I absolutely abhorred the thought of being treated like a child with my own husband act-ing as my parent. But if I was going to follow Jesus, the rebellion brewing inside of me had to be subdued. I took a deep breath, hum-bled myself, and asked his forgiveness for touching the dial without his permission, then waited for him to reciprocate. He didn't say a word. I prodded, "So . . . are you going to apologize for slapping me in the face, because that was really uncalled for?" "Nope," he said, "because you had it coming." I had it coming? Really? Was it in the misogynistic handbook or something, and I just missed it? It's one thing to simply forgive and let it go. But it's another to be a doormat. I decided that I had nothing more to say to him until he admitted he was wrong, so we finished out the day in silence as I wrestled with anger and grief, reliving in my mind the litany of crippling things he had said and done in our five months of marriage, all the while preparing for ministry. When it was time to go to sleep, I couldn't bring myself to get in the tent, so I remained outside, contemplating my options. Realizing I wasn't joining him, Troy made a snide remark, threw my pillow at me, zipped up the tent door, and went to sleep. I sat out under the stars, weeping uncontrollably, as I had never felt more alone and abandoned.

The next day, the thick silence continued. By the afternoon, Troy finally spoke. "I know you want me to apologize," he said, dripping with sarcasm, "so here it goes. I'm sorry for living. I'm sorry for breathing. I'm sorry for everything in the world there is to be sorry for. Now are you happy?" Wow! Way to cover his bases. He had offered a blanket apology to cover every offense ever committed. Brilliant! Should I have thanked him profusely for going above and beyond what I had even asked? I didn't want to accept his lame, dumbass apology at all, but what choice did I have? I concluded that God was allowing this so that I could learn how to forgive freely. I swallowed the bitter pill of injustice, reluctantly accepted his snarky attempt at reconciliation, and quietly thanked God once again for the amazing work He was doing in my heart.

27

Out of Control

The issue was deeper than a slap in the face or touching the radio dial. The underlying force behind nearly every fight or struggle was Troy's need to be in control. As much as I wanted to help set up camp or load and unload the car, I wasn't allowed because I couldn't do it "correctly." At the same time, I was criticized for just standing around. The "no touch" rule applied to virtually everything in the car, but especially his Indiana Jones hat that he was afraid I might bend or warp in some way. One time, I picked it up to prevent it from getting squished while the car was being loaded, and he came unglued. "What part of 'Don't touch my stuff' do you not understand?" When I boldly suggested that he was being just a wee bit too anal about the hat, he became furious and threw it in the Dumpster to make me feel guilty. "There! Are you happy now?" he scolded. "The hat is gone! You've gotten your wish! Now you can stop your pathetic whining!" There was nothing about the encounter that even resembled "whining," but somehow, any vocalization on my part that differed from his point of view was heard as such. I retrieved it from the trash and put it back in the car because I couldn't bear to have him blame me for its demise, but he refused to ever wear it again.

He reacted similarly when I offered to take a turn driving. Since we were traveling thousands of miles over the course of the summer, I thought it would be a pleasant change for both of us to trade spots occasionally, but each time I asked, he refused. Now I can assume that the reader might at least wonder if Troy's assessment of me being a nagging bitch had at least an ounce of merit. That's a fair question. All I can say is I was reluctant to make a request of any type and preemptively rehearsed in my head multiple times what I wanted to say before it ever left my lips. The conversation would typically go like this:

"Hey Troy, I'm happy to drive for a while and give you a break."

"No, I can drive."

"Okay."

Another day: "Troy, you know, I wouldn't mind driving. It might be a nice change to trade spots."

"No, that's okay. I can do it."

"Okay."

A week later: "Troy, I was thinking maybe I could drive for a little while sometime today. What do you think?"

"No. I'll drive."

At that point, I wasn't sure if he thought I was just being nice to offer to drive or if he thought I was asking permission. So I worked up the courage, after practicing under my breath, to seek clarification of the situation. I timidly asked, "Is there a reason you don't want me to drive?" The next thing I knew, the car was swerving dramatically to the shoulder, as if dodging a deer or an illegal alien at border crossing. Troy slammed on the brakes, lurching the car to an unnatural stop, got out, and demanded that I start driving since I wanted to "sooo badly." The invitation felt more like a terrifying carjacking at gunpoint, and I was no longer in the mood. He was trying to make me feel guilty and ashamed simply for asking. I didn't know if I was supposed to obey him and start driving, even though he clearly didn't want me to or recant and say I had changed my mind. Stuffing down my own unworthiness, I reluctantly put the car in gear. But I had no idea where we were or even where we were going. He controlled the map because I couldn't read it fast enough to his satisfaction. "Troy, can you please tell me which way to go?" I asked weakly.

"Not my problem. You wanted to drive," he retorted smugly, as he turned his face toward the passenger door." With that, he acted like he was going to hunker down and sleep. Damn! I knew he had won, and so, with silent resignation, I relinquished my five minutes in the driver's seat and returned it to the rightful owner, never to usurp his authority in that way again.

I'm not sure how well I saw the patterns at the time, but through reliving the stories, I can better understand Troy's reactions. If he perceived that I wanted to share control, he would pretend to give it to me but would sabotage it so I would fail and he could go back to being in charge, as in my request to drive. If I expressed that I was dissatisfied or uncomfortable with something that was happening, he would give me what I wanted but in such an exaggerated way, so that my request looked silly. For example, if I mentioned that I was nervous about us getting a speeding ticket, he might slow down to thirty-five miles an hour on the freeway so cars would be honking and blaring past us and then refuse to speed up, insisting that he was only "giving me what I wanted." Other manipulation tactics included shaming, mockery, belittling, name calling, withholding affection, blaming, trivializing my concerns, intimidation, violence, and invalidating my feelings by equating me to a spoiled, petulant child for even the most benign requests.

Essentially, I had no voice, and if I attempted to exercise any autonomy, I was shut down and mercilessly shamed. If I expressed a need, he took it personally as a criticism and became deeply offended, unable to put himself in my shoes. It may seem selfish on my part to have stayed in a relationship, believing my husband didn't love me. Why didn't I cut my losses and take the next bus home and free him from his obligation? But it wasn't that simple. The passive-aggressive signals were confusing. When confessing that I felt unloved by his blatant rejection, he would imply that the problem was with me and not him. My expectations were just too high, or I was just too sensitive.

"I give and I give, but it's never enough for you!" he would say, making me feel that even my most basic, primal requests were ridiculous and frivolous. So if he did love me and I was just too demanding or unable to interpret the clues accurately, the solution was for me to try harder and expect less, not get a divorce. In hindsight, I can see that Troy exhibited many of the markers for borderline personality and narcissistic disorder. His profound lack of empathy and insatiable need for control were dead giveaways. But at the time, my only framework for analyzing situations was the Bible, and I believed God was using our marriage to sanctify us for our good and His glory.

At the end of the summer, after earning additional gas and food money along the way through odd jobs at Troy's parents' ranch in Montana, we had $100 to our name when we landed in Pasadena, California, the end of the line. Troy visited the campus of Fuller Theological Seminary and decided it was a perfect fit. The wife slapper was going to be a pastor. We unloaded the car, settled into our tiny studio apartment as assistant managers in exchange for free rent, and started over, with all our original "baggage" plus some extra we had accumulated along the way still in tow.

28

Catch 22

Even in beautiful, sunny California with palm trees and sandy beaches, I could see that Troy's happy meter was barely registering, and I knew it was my fault. I continued to forsake my own desires for his good and would've done almost anything for him if it meant that he wouldn't act so disappointed to call me his wife. I tried to understand what he needed. He didn't need physical affection. His incessant pushing me away told me that what he needed was space. So I gave him as much berth as I could muster. I learned to sleep on the very edge of the bed, making little movement, with my back to him so as not to touch him in the night. I learned to keep a full body's distance from him on the couch. He couldn't tolerate neediness in any form, so I would literally go for weeks, tiptoeing around him, trying not to make waves or give him any reason to think of me as a tiresome wench. Even during sex, I didn't dare ask him to help me climax because I feared it would be the straw that broke the camel's back. As much as I longed for him to hold me, hug me, kiss me, or do anything to offer some emotional validation, I couldn't express it because I didn't want to be rejected for being perceived as weak. Instead I would go for walks and pray my heart out, convincing myself that God's love was all I needed. That would work, for the most part, but every once in a while, especially when I was hormonal, it wasn't enough to be loved by my imaginary friend. I needed a real person made of flesh to touch me and assure me that I too wasn't invisible.

One evening, when I was feeling particularly vulnerable, I reluctantly asked Troy if I could have a good night kiss. As Troy lay with his back toward me on the futon mattress we had on the floor, he refused, saying, "Why do *I* have to give *you* a kiss? If you want one so badly, you can just give me one." I tried to explain that it wasn't the act of kissing that I needed. It was the act of *being* kissed that made me feel loved in that moment. I wanted to be pursued. Then the mocking started. "Oh boo-hoo! Is poor little Joy not getting enough attention? Is mean ole Troy hurting her feelings again?" Still he just lay there, stubborn and unyielding. Hurt by his ridiculing, I slapped him on his back and said, "I honestly don't know how to communicate in a way that I feel heard. I'm telling you what I need and you won't even roll over and look at me." With that, I headed to the closet to pull out a blanket with the intent of sleeping in the hallway, since the studio apartment left few options. In an instant, his apathy turned into rage as he jumped up, followed me, and violently slammed the sliding closet door shut just as I instinctively yanked my arm away to avoid getting it crushed. He grabbed me so hard that his finger marks were left on my arms as bruises, and he shoved me back onto the mattress, sat on top of me, covering my mouth and nose with his hand, and screamed, "You are nothing but a nagging bitch, and I can't do anything to please you!" I kicked and fought, trying to get him to move his hand from my nose and mouth because I couldn't breathe, but he only pressed harder and shouted louder, "Shut up! I said, shut up! Shut up, you bitch!" It was only when I stopped resisting and went limp that he finally moved his hand and I could gasp for air. I'd never been more terrified in my life and believed he was going to kill me. When he was satisfied that he had subdued me, he gave me a hug, much like a parent would after disciplining a child, and said, "This was for your own good." Then turned his back toward me again, without so much as an apology, as I wept silently in my pillow.

The very next day, my parents, who had finally forgiven me after months of letters and phone calls affirming my love for them, showed up with the car and belongings we had left in Missouri. I confided in Mom that I was frightened of Troy, revealing the tender bruises on my arms. Mom told Dad, and Dad was livid. He was about to threaten Troy within an inch of his life, but Mom made him promise not to get involved because she didn't want to make things worse for me. So in the middle of the night, my parents simply vanished without saying goodbye, and I was left to carry on, as if nothing had happened. I didn't know to whom I could turn, so I reached out to friends at church. I tried to hint that Troy was being abusive but was promptly rebuked for putting my husband in a negative light. In Christian terms, I was guilty of "gossiping" and was admonished to share only what was lovely and of a good report (Philippians 4:8). Since there was no "good report" category for domestic violence, I could find no acceptable avenue to discuss it, and so it necessarily became my own silent burden.

Despite my efforts to absolve Troy of any responsibility or obligation, we continued drifting further apart. I was slowly building a fortress of self-protection to keep from being constantly harmed by his physical, emotional, and verbal abuse. And his perceived "needs" were just barricades keeping us from being anything more than roommates. By agreeing to his selfish demands, I was contributing to the dysfunction of our relationship. It was a Catch 22, and no matter what I did, I couldn't win.

The reality of the situation was that I was in a loveless marriage, and I imagine most couples would've seen the handwriting on the wall and called it quits long before it had reached this point. Yet I was absolutely convinced that God was using all of this to prepare us for future ministry. God was teaching me to find my source of joy and comfort in him, regardless of Troy's words and actions. I thanked God every day for my trials and praised him for the "spiritual maturity" he was building in Troy and me. The mark of true discipleship was to endure pain, injustice, and suffering without so much as a whimper. When Jesus was dying on the cross, he said, "Father, forgive them. They know not what they do." If this model was good enough for Jesus, then surely, as his follower, it was good enough for me.

29

Bride of Christ

Over the years, Christianity had mostly been about following rules, repenting of sins, getting right with Jesus, bracing myself for the Rapture, and pursuing holiness through spiritual disciplines such as prayer, Bible study, and witnessing. I knew Jesus would reward me with eternal life when I died, but in the meantime, the here and now was about sacrifice and pain and being found worthy, with occasional rewards to whet my appetite for heaven.

But the face of Christianity changed when we walked into Abundant Life Community Church in Pasadena, California. This cult was nothing like anything we had ever encountered, and after only one service, we were completely hooked. The people were real and unpretentious. Some wore flip-flops and shorts to church in place of traditional dresses and suit jackets. Others brought their knitting to multitask during the sermon. More expressive individuals, including men, secure in their masculinity, did interpretive dance off to the side during worship while others remained seated in contemplative meditation. Che, the Korean American pastor, openly divulged his own shortcomings as he tried to lead the congregation, by example, into a lifestyle of honest humility. Macaroni salad, tater-tot casseroles, and fried chicken graced the tables in the meeting hall every Thursday night where the members gathered together for a potluck meal, called a Love Feast, to enjoy fellowship and get to know one another. Their mission was to follow the model of the first New Testament Christians who shared everything they had with each other. It was like one big giant commune, and I had never seen so much freedom and pure love and joy expressed as I did at Abundant Life. I jumped in with reckless abandon, playing the piano on the worship team, teaching Sunday school, writing children's musicals, attending small group meetings, and joining women's Bible studies. Troy and I were embraced immediately, and when we were at church, it seemed that our marital failings and hurts momentarily melted away.

One Sunday morning, I had an epiphany. I was not only married to Troy, but I was married to Jesus as well. I was, in fact, the "bride of Christ." Troy was incapable of providing the love and emotional support that I needed. He had his own issues to work through, and as much as I wanted him to be there for me, he simply couldn't. But my other lover, Jesus, could. He could minister to me through His "body," the church. Okay, I admit, it sounds creepy when I say it out loud. In a spiritual sense, though, I saw the church as the tangible, embodiment of Jesus. Because I was accepted and cherished at Abundant Life, I could bear the agony of going home night after night and being ignored, belittled, and marginalized.

30

Fake It 'Til You Make It

When we first got married, I thought it would be fun to record how many times we made love through the course of our marriage so that we could reveal the stats on our fiftieth anniversary with a guessing jar of candy kisses. Our first year (the honeymoon phase), I had recorded fifty-four tallies. I realize some lovers meet this quota after only a month or so, but we got off to a rocky start and I was confident we would eventually get our stride. However, by the second year, we were down to twelve, and by the third year, I threw out the book, because I didn't need the glaring reminder that our marriage was in crisis and that I might in fact, be recording a countdown to divorce.

It was my birthday, and Troy was at school. I had made a platter of cheese and crackers and bought a cheap bottle of champagne to celebrate when he got home. Trying to gauge everything just right, based on his estimated time of arrival, I lit the room with candles, creating a romantic ambiance, and waited. But he didn't show up. We had so little money to spare, and even this small gesture was a taxing burden on our budget. An hour passed and then two and then three. The cheese plate was warm. My special plan was evaporating along with the disappearing candle wax. *Screw him!* I thought. *I don't need him to celebrate my birthday. I don't need him to hug me or love me or even fuck me. I'm in charge of my own happiness*, I convinced myself, as the tears escaping down my face seemed to undermine my defiant resolve. The church was there for me when it came to social events and book groups. But it couldn't be with me in the bedroom. That was the one thing only Troy could offer, and when he didn't, I had to convince myself that I didn't care. I struggled to pop the cork on the substandard Cook's Grand Reserve, and when I finally succeeded, I started guzzling as only a novice connoisseur could. For the first and only time in my life, I downed the entire bottle, numbing the disappointment of sitting alone on my birthday with no one to acknowledge that I mattered. In my stupor, I began to feel the dissolution of hope that things would ever be different. I was weary of feeling constantly rejected and incapable of making Troy happy. I allowed myself to toy with the idea of a legal separation, since divorce would never be a part of our vocabulary, but figured such crazy talk was just the alcohol clouding my thinking. I was sure I would feel differently when the buzz wore off. He still wasn't home when I went to bed, and so I fell asleep, intoxicated and wallowing in self-pity.

But just as my last morsel of hope had slipped through my fingers, Troy managed to keep a faint ember still burning. He was a master at driving me away and then suddenly doing something nice to prove that my hurt feelings were unjustified. The next day, he presented me with a jewelry box, proof that I was wrong to accuse him of not caring. I don't recall where he was the night before or why he didn't come home as planned. I just remember the gift accompanied by a rebuke, and I felt ashamed for being hurt and angry. His kind gesture kept my restless feelings at bay for a little while, but it wasn't long before they were taking up residence again in my thoughts. One night I had a dream, and in it, I was told, "Life is short." I woke up trying to interpret this message through my spiritual decoder lenses. I wondered if God was telling me that life was too short to live day by day without being loved. I went to the pastors and shared with them what I was contemplating. Of course, they were sure that my interpretation was misguided at best. Their translation was that because life is short, no matter how awful it is, it will be over in a blink and we will enjoy heaven for all eternity. So in the meantime, we should rejoice in our light and momentary afflictions, knowing that we are storing up riches in heaven. I concurred that their prophetic assessment was more accurate, and I knew I couldn't throw in the towel. God was still working on us, and I just needed to be patient.

Lou, one of the pastors on staff, offered us some free counseling. "Do you love Troy?" he asked directly. Without hesitating, I answered, "Yes, I love him very much, but I simply don't know how to make him happy." And then Lou asked Troy, "Do you love Joy?" Troy paused for a few seconds, shook his head, and scrunched up his face. "No, not really," he said, in the same cadence he might respond to the question "Would you like some leftover meatloaf?" I knew it. I knew it. I knew it! As difficult as it was to hear, I was so relieved that he was finally able to admit the truth. The elephant in the room stood up and confidently trumpeted its presence, demanding to be acknowledged. He confessed that he felt pressure from family and friends to get married after Bible college because that's what everyone did. His real dream had been to join a monastery and live a life of celibate devotion to God. At least he wasn't longing for someone else who was prettier, sexier, or able to do crazy human contortions in bed. My only competition was a convent for men! My gut sense had been right all along, but my distorted lens had kept me trapped in a fantasy world of false hope and denial. But now that the truth was out, it seemed that the most logical, compassionate, and reasonable solution would be to set each other free and move on. We had no children. We were still very young. It made sense. But Christian counseling isn't always practical, and it doesn't take into consideration *reality*! It's about following the Bible, despite the circumstances. The pastor instead encouraged us to fake it 'til we make it. I mean, what's love got to do with it anyway, right? We were assigned the task of going for a walk every day and holding hands. And before we went to sleep, we were to kiss each other and say, "I love you." Of all the difficult things I was asked to do as a believer, like go door to door witnessing, become a social outcast, join an intercessory prayer chain, wear Jesus buttons, or read Leviticus, this by far, was the hardest. How could I possibly feel even the least bit okay with holding hands and kissing a person who didn't want to be with me? Of course, it was exactly what I had been doing all along, but until now, I had been grasping on to the fragment of hope that my instincts were wrong. Intimacy is the sacred by-product of a beautiful emotional and sexual connection, something we had never possessed, even from the beginning. The last thing I wanted was to be treated like a mandatory homework assignment, and yet I knew I had to swallow my pride and simply go through the motions as instructed by my spiritual shepherd. My feelings were irrelevant. Obedience was paramount. With my spiritual glasses, I could see a hint of happiness on the horizon but not without a painful purging of my will. I had to die to self, just as Christ had to die on the cross. This is what Jesus meant when he said, "If you want to be my disciple, you must take up your cross and follow me." A loveless marriage, I concluded, was my cross to bear, if I was to be conformed to the image of Christ. I had no choice but to embrace God's "perfect" will with joy.

Part IV

The Great Commission

"Go Ye Into All the World and Make Disciples"

31

Missionary Position

I believed our marriage was improving because we were following the prescribed checklist, even though the feelings to back up our actions didn't match. I didn't know what to compare our relationship to because we had never had a "normal" loving marriage, so just to have it at least functional was, in my mind, a step in the right direction, and I saw this as proof of God's faithfulness. For a couple of years, we were cordial roommates, tiptoeing on eggshells around each other, careful not to step on any landmines that might blow up our fragile façade.

One day, Troy's best friend, Brad, from Trinity, called and invited us to work with him for a year in Taipei, Taiwan. Brad was filling in for a missionary who was returning to the States on furlough and asked if Troy wanted to come over and give him a hand. Troy was getting his Master of Divinity with a cross-cultural emphasis at Fuller Seminary and needed to do an internship. Serving as a missionary for a year would be perfect. We took a job as house parents for mentally challenged adults in exchange for free room and board, and I taught second grade at a Christian school in Los Angeles (where Richard Thomas's, a.k.a. John Boy Walton's, triplet daughters attended) to help pay for our one-way plane ticket to Taiwan. Once again, I was optimistic that this move to the other side of the world would be our golden ticket. We could leave our troubles behind and start over together. I surmised that the only reason we weren't prospering was because we weren't in ministry together! That was it! Once we started fulfilling the great commission, "going into all the world to preach the Gospel," God would surely knit our hearts together. Infused with a resurgence of faith and renewed vision, I welcomed our new beginning as missionaries, working toward a common goal—saving the lost and, at the same time, salvaging our marriage.

Before I jump ahead to our missionary endeavors in Taiwan, I need to pause temporarily and share about our experience taking care of mentally disabled adults because, after all, who doesn't like to hear a good masturbation story! Just kidding (sort of). While working with these special needs adults, I was faced with another theological conundrum where Christianity and reality seemed to be at odds. I had been taught and firmly believed that the Bible contained objective, universal morality for all people in all times—past, present, and future. If something was deemed a sin when the Bible was written, it was still a sin two thousand years later and was no respecter of persons. And as I had been faithfully taught, I believed the wage of sin is death and everyone is guilty as charged. The solution is to gain forgiveness and receive eternal life by putting one's faith in Jesus and repenting of all known sins. But then I met Greg, an eight-year-old mind in a twenty-three-year-old body who lived in the group home where we were house parents. Greg was a friendly guy who lived in a virtual world created from his imagination. When he would come to church with us, he would either pretend that I was his wife or spin a tragic story of losing his family in a car accident or some such disaster. We never knew what far-fetched tale would escape his lips, but church members quickly caught on and allowed him his delusional fantasies. Besides his propensity to tell outlandish whoppers, he also had one rather embarrassing and compulsive habit of masturbating, even in public. Every time I looked at him, he had his hand either in his pants or on the outside, juggling his balls like a circus performer. I'm sure he fantasized nightly and daily using the poster above his bed of a scantily clad woman, while soaking up the gallons of accumulated semen with his crusty sheets. He couldn't help himself. But masturbation was supposed to be a sin, not to mention lying, which he did daily. He knew his stories weren't true and would sheepishly apologize when confronted. Was Greg sinning if he couldn't help it? How could he be accountable when his mental capacity was so severely compromised? And then there was sweet Mary, who was just smart enough to realize she was mentally disabled. She couldn't handle the stigma and tragically hanged herself. Isn't suicide a mortal sin? Another girl, Sheila, struggled with alcohol abuse and solicited sex in public restrooms. Her parents had her sterilized so that she wouldn't get pregnant. According to the Bible, all these behaviors committed by adults with diminished mental capacities were serious sins, worthy of God's wrath. But I simply couldn't imagine God condemning them when he was responsible for limiting their IQs. So what was I to make of it? Does God simply overlook some sins if a person is incapable of making better choices? The implication would be that the plan of salvation is different for some. In other words, "Believe, confess, and repent" is not a universal blueprint for heaven. Mentally disabled people, babies, unborn fetuses, schizophrenics, and elderly with Alzheimer's are all people to whom the Gospel would have to look differently. It posed a theological dilemma with regards to my understanding of Jesus dying for our sins and only being able to allocate forgiveness to those who, by their own free will, asked for it. If he could simply save people outside of free will, then everyone on the planet could potentially be saved by God's prerogative. And if that were true, why would anyone need to believe in Jesus and repent of his or her sins to gain eternal life as the Bible clearly stated? I conveniently tucked this paradox away in a separate compartment so that I could continue to believe what I had always been taught without this enigma unraveling my perfect doctrine. Any piece that didn't seem to fit was thrown into my theological junk drawer to be sorted later.

32

The Mission Field

Taipei, Taiwan, was uncharted territory in every sense of the word; Any shred of familiarity or comfort was completely swallowed up by the vast strangeness that engulfed us the moment we stepped off the plane. It was a unique blend of old-world charm and new-world industrialism, with giant skyscrapers and neon-lighted signs and little old women wearing their traditional woven cone hat, sweeping the street with a straw broom across six lanes of traffic. We were clearly the minority and felt like illiterate little children, unable to read the street signs or billboards. Not only that, I was like a supersize Big Mac in a vast sea of children's happy meals. I went shopping for a pair of dress slacks, and when the clerk, with her tape measure, sized up my 5'5", 128-pound frame, she acted like she had never seen numbers quite so large. "Okay. No probrem. Try these pant over here. They reary, reary big. They fit you! Just try!" The last thing I wanted to hear was that I needed "reary reary" big pants. I guess it was just another lesson in humility, as if all the other lessons were not enough.

The missionary who had returned to the States on furlough had assured us that we would have plenty to do during our stint in Taipei. In addition to worship services on Sunday, he also had a daily radio program running in which we could host, as well as a language school and a monthly magazine that we could write for and distribute. The radio, language school, and magazine were all positions that would earn an income to subsidize our stay. Typically, missionaries raise support in their local churches before going abroad, but we didn't take that route since we knew we could earn our own keep. But leaving the airport, Brad said, "Oh, by the way. Just to let you know, none of the programs are up and running, so you'll need to find work elsewhere while you are here." Just to reiterate, we had a one-way ticket to a foreign country with no money and no home in which to return. *And*, if we wanted to stay, we had to find our own jobs! But with my childlike faith, I knew God had called us there, and I was certain He would prove himself faithful even on the other side of the world. I couldn't wait to see how the miracle would unfold.

33

The Miracle

We had been in Taipei for three days when the "miracle" happened. Brad and Troy were off working at the church and I was home alone in the apartment. The phone rang for the first time since we had arrived. I stood staring at it, frozen, wondering whether or not to answer it, because if the caller spoke Chinese, I wouldn't know what to say. But it kept ringing, and finally I picked up the receiver and nervously said, "Wei?" (Hello.) The caller said, "Hello, I'm looking for Joy Corbin. Do you know how I might reach her?" I nearly dropped the phone. I had been in town three days and someone speaking English was asking for me. Puzzled, I responded, "This is Joy speaking." "Oh, wonderful!" the person said. "This is Lois from Taipei American School. You sent us a job application several months ago, which we still have on file. We were wondering if you would like to come in this week for an interview. One of our teachers had a family emergency and needed to return to the States. Are you still interested or available?" There was at least a three-second lag between her words and my brain's processing speed. Slowly I stammered, "I . . . uh . . . well . . . yes! Absolutely! I would love to come in for an interview. But I'm sorry. I just have to ask. How did you find me? We arrived here only a few days ago and don't even know my own phone number!" She explained that on my application, I stated that my husband was doing missionary work. So she decided to go through the list of missionary agencies in alphabetical order to find me, and our number was listed with the Assemblies of God, which

happened to be the first name on the list. She too was pleasantly surprised that she had found me on her first try! I was convinced I had
just experienced a miracle. The process of finding me through deduc-
tive reasoning was replaced in my mind with something more akin to
"Lois opened the phone book, closed her eyes, spun her finger in the
air, landed on a number, opened her eyes, spat in the air three times,
and voila! She found me!" But regardless, the fact remained that I
needed a job. I wanted to teach, and the school where I had applied
to months earlier simultaneously needed a teacher. Make no mistake!
This was more than a coincidence. This had God's fingerprints all
over it! Just like our rhyming names, our synchronized relocation to
Springfield, and the reunion with my birth family, this new miracle
was yet another sign from God that despite all the bumps and heartache, we were in His perfect will.

34

Jingle Bells and Other Worship Hits

Returning to the Assemblies of God after leaving to join People of Destiny, Abundant Life's affiliation, made me remember why I hated it so much and had no desire to return. Troy was immediately criticized for his long hair and ear piercing. If he was going to work in the church, he would be forced to get a haircut and remove the earring to "look like a real Christian." Troy, resenting having others tell him what to do, kicked up his heels in protest, but in order to stay and complete his internship, he eventually was forced to comply. Despite our theological differences, we were ready to jump in, serve the church, and do our part to advance the gospel.

The Chinese service was quiet, controlled, and rather stoic. Because the sermons were in Chinese, I didn't usually attend, since the extent of my Mandarin included counting to ten, a greeting, an introduction, and some completely useless phrases such as "The little man is on the big bus," none of which helped illuminate the sermon. The English service picked up the pace and volume a bit, with more charismatic worship, lifting hands during prayer, and speaking in tongues. I played the piano and selected the music for the worship team during this service. But the Filipino church was where all the excitement was. They were loud, boisterous, emotional, and very much like a room full of bouncy Tiggers. Their exuberance was downright contagious as they would clap and bop up and down while worshipping. One time the entire congregation had their hands up in the air, passionately singing, "Joy is the flag flown high from the castle of my heart." Suddenly, midstream, the pianist broke into "Dashing through the snow in a one-horse open sleigh," and they didn't miss a beat. With their hands still extended to heaven, they continued to praise Jesus, as if "Jingle Bells" was actually extolling the virtues of the Most High. When Brad gave an altar call, encouraging people to get saved, the Filipinos would literally grab their neighbors and drag or push them to the front against their will to repent of their sins. One day during an altar call, the pianist, who was also a nightclub performer, started singing, "I'm dreaming of a white Christmas" in pure Bing Crosby flare, and people started crying and coming forward for salvation. The famous agnostic composer, Irving Berlin, who wrote the nostalgic song, likely never dreamed that his secular hit would be used to convert Filipinos to Christianity! I tried not to think too hard about what I was witnessing because just under the surface of my seemingly impenetrable faith shield were some tiny seeds of doubt that if nurtured could wreak havoc in my spiritual garden. I wanted to believe all this craziness was the working of the Holy Spirit, but I couldn't help but feel a bit skeptical. I did my best to squelch the nagging suspicion that our entire worship experience was fueled merely by group dynamics and chord patterns manipulating our heartstrings. I looked to scripture for some rationalization. Jesus said that if we didn't worship Him, even the rocks and hills would cry out. I speculated, if God could be worshipped by gravel, then surely he wouldn't mind songs about sleigh bells and snowy winters either. So I tried to put my nagging doubts to rest, suppressing them at best.

Questions continued to mount though, as I attended the English services. I cringed when people would speak in tongues and someone else would give the interpretation. After observing people barking like dogs and simulating epileptic seizures in the name of the Holy Ghost, over the years, I was justifiably cautious. Since "tongues" aren't a real language, it's impossible to prove whether or not the interpretation is from God. If it sounded at all like something Jesus *might* say, I would give them the benefit of the doubt. But sometimes, it was obvious that the message was not divinely inspired.

For example, one time, a middle-aged white ex-patriot stood up to translate a woman's channeled gibberish. His slurred speech was a dead giveaway that his interpretation had probably been influenced more by JD (Jack Daniels) rather than JC.

He started with, "You are all lazy, good-for-nothing bums, saith the Lord. What are you doing for my kingdom? saith the Lord. What are you doing for my church? saith the Lord." Usually, when someone was on a roll, people would be cheering and shouting, "Amen. Yes, Lord! Speak to us, Lord!" The congregation started to echo their affirmations until his words caught up with their brains. Then everyone fell silent, in confusion and wonderment. The prophet continued, "You all need to get off your big fat asses and start doing something for me. [belch] Thus saith the Lord! *Glorydagod!* Amen." A few feeble claps bounced off the walls but quickly ceased when the rest of the congregation failed to follow suit. It was as if everyone was secretly thinking, "What the hell was that?" The pastor, who was a marvelous spin doctor, though, somehow rendered the scathing, booze-induced rebuke credible, and people wept, begging God to forgive them for their lukewarm faith. I, however, wasn't convinced. If people could fake it, how would one ever know what was real?

Our one-year assignment turned into two, and during my time in Taiwan, my faith came perilously close to crumbling. Had we stayed another year, I wonder if it would've collapsed altogether. My biggest spiritual crisis stemmed from contemplating the reality that out of twenty million people in Taiwan, only 2 percent of the population were Christian. If the Bible was true, that meant 19,600,000 of Taiwanese were doomed for hell. Men, women, children, grandparents, teachers, street sweepers, fruit vendors, craftsmen, doctors, and chefs were all going to be tortured forever in a lake of fire. It would be one thing if these had been deplorable, selfish predators, raping children and robbing old ladies. But no, instead, they were uncharacteristically gentle, humble, and peace-loving. I remembered back in sixth grade, grappling with the death of Judy Pohipe, my resident bully, and being grief-stricken that she was suffering in hell, and I didn't even like her. Then I thought of Greg, Mary, and Sheila, the mentally disabled adults, and thought, *How terribly unfortunate and unfair if they were tossed in the flames.* Now I was faced with the same dilemma, only this time, dealing with an entire culture! I couldn't fathom how many billions of people worldwide would be cast into hell and how few would make it to heaven because they had been taught a different faith tradition. This just couldn't be right! I couldn't help but think, *There has to be a loophole somewhere. How could God be satisfied with getting 2 percent on his side, while letting Satan have 98 percent?* Even if there was a mass revival and every person in Taiwan was miraculously saved through the efforts of two young white missionaries from Pasadena with rhyming names, there would still be the billions from previous generations who had never heard the "Good News." The Christian message wasn't standardized and universal. It seemed to only apply to a certain group of people whose IQ, ethnicity, geographical location, and family history made it possible for them to accept Jesus as their savior. The only way I could possibly reconcile my faith with this horrible reality was to trust that God, who is all-loving and all-merciful, would find a way to save them, even if He was to speak to them on their deathbed directly and give them a chance. This was another mystery I would cram into my theological junk drawer to find a permanent home for later. But down deep, my faith was starting to hemorrhage. The pieces just weren't adding up. The apologists' answer to my faith crisis offered only superficial comfort, but I latched onto it nonetheless. "God's ways," they said, "are so far outside of our human intellect that we can't even begin to understand!" I tried not to think about it and simply left the fate of Taipei in the hands of my white, western, Republican God.

35

Third Wheel

For the first time in four years, I saw Troy appear to be somewhat happy. Nothing in our relationship had changed. In fact, we were as distant as ever, both physically and emotionally. The difference was Brad.

Being reunited with his best friend brought Troy back to the glory days of Trinity when he was carefree and single. He and Brad had worked in student government together for four years. Now they were picking up where they had left off in Taiwan. The three of us shared an apartment, and by all appearances, it was more like Brad and Troy were the couple and I was the third wheel. For example, when we rode in Brad's car, he and Troy took the front seat while I rode alone in the back. They also worked closely at the church and went out with students on Friday nights to strike up conversations about Christianity. I joined them a couple of times but was too exhausted from my own work schedule to continue. And long after I would be in bed, they would stay up watching movies together in the living room. Other times, they would stay out until two or three in the morning, hanging out at nightclubs where the Filipinos from the church performed, without ever calling to let me know they were safe. I wondered if it was possible that Troy was gay but either couldn't admit or didn't realize it, since there was no room within Christianity for him explore such feelings. Many of my California friends had speculated about this as well, and Troy's closeness with

Brad only confirmed the possibility. This would certainly explain his frigid emotional and physical detachment from me.

Our dream of going to Taiwan to do ministry together and to grow closer as a couple was not being realized. We were two people in Taiwan doing completely different things and functionally living separate lives. It was Brad and Troy who had formed the ministry partnership and who were essentially being the missionaries in Taipei, and I was the silent third-party financier who paid the rent. The kindling flame I had hoped to ignite produced only a few sputtering sparks and then died out, leaving me to feel cold and alienated yet again, with no family within a twenty-hour plane ride to comfort me.

36

So Tell Me What You Really Think!

One night, when Troy and Brad were out doing their thing and I was home alone, feeling jilted, in the apartment, I noticed Troy's journal lying on the bed. Yes, I confess, I peeked in it. Don't judge. Besides, you're probably dying to know if I discovered evidence of Troy's sexual orientation. Am I right? Sexual preference aside, I just wanted to know what, if anything, Troy was saying about *me*. On one hand, he appeared to show no restraint in arguing a point or demanding his way, but when asked about his feelings, he was bottled up tight, with a wife-proof safety cap, refusing to divulge what was going on inside. This was another way he kept himself distanced from me, and I desperately wanted to know the real story, especially as it related to our relationship. After talking myself out of it for several minutes, my better judgment finally crumbled under pressure, and my curiosity swooped in, like a renegade military coup.

Nervously, I opened the book and began to skim the pages for my name. There it was.

"Joy is so demanding—has to have immediate gratification or she throws a fit."

"Joy is wishy-washy."

"Joy pressured me to get married."

"I'll never be a pastor with Joy in the picture."

"Marriage gets harder and harder all the time."

"Why did I get married?"

"Death is so inviting."

"Now what?"

"No real love."

"I think I'm in love with Brad." Just kidding. He didn't say that.

One of the most utterly frustrating traits that Troy exhibited, even from day one of our marriage, was to assume to know what I was thinking and to assign motives to my actions. If I expressed something that contradicted his inferences, he would go so far as accuse me of lying rather than adjust his assumptions, and there was not a thing I could do about it to ever change his mind. For example, one Saturday afternoon, Troy, Brad, and I visited the National Palace Museum in Taipei. The stress and exhaustion from the week had caught up to me, and I found myself tired, a bit dizzy, and nursing a throbbing headache. After about forty-five minutes of looking at the exhibits, I decided I would cut the trip short, grab a taxi home, and take a nap. I assured Troy that I didn't need or want him to come with me and that he should stay and enjoy the museum for as long as he wanted with Brad, and I would meet him back at the apartment later. But this was Troy's version chronicled in his journal.

> Joy faked a headache today [false assumption] because she doesn't like museums [false assumption]. I wish she wouldn't lie about it [false assumption]. Then she said she wanted to get a cab and that she didn't need me go with her, but I knew better [false assumption]. If I didn't go with her she would probably throw a fit [false assumption], so I had to leave the museum early [false conclusion].

By believing and acting upon his own version of reality and ignoring my actual words and intentions, he could continue to perpetuate the "me" that he had crafted from his own disturbed imagination. Consequently, the narrow little box that he put me in remained fastened and secure despite my emphatic protests to be let out. This was yet another way his narcissistic control manifested itself.

Through all the pages, I couldn't find one nice or empathetic thing about me or us as a couple. Nothing. Not a single word. My wishful thinking that he really did appreciate me but didn't know how to show it proved to be just that, wishful thinking, and my heart began to ache with inconsolable grief. The tears started to trickle down my cheeks when I read about his fantasy of emptying our savings account and just disappearing. He was a caged tiger dreaming of escape—from me, the annoying, lying, wishy-washy, demanding monkey on his back. Had I been in a healthier place emotionally and had I not already felt completely unlovable, Troy's criticism of me could've been brushed off like a sprinkling of dandruff on the shoulder of my Dad's '80s paisley suit jacket he wore every Sunday. Perhaps I could've even laughed at his ridiculous faultfinding. But instead, the words stung like the welt-producing whip on my bare bottom when I was a kid. What is God trying to show me or teach me? The mantra I had been saying for several years again reminded me that I deserved nothing except hell. My greatest need was satisfied when Jesus died on the cross and paved the way for me to receive eternal life. Therefore, I didn't need nor did I deserve for Troy to have a high opinion of me. I only "needed" Jesus. But in Taipei, Jesus felt a million miles away. I longed to be back home, being loved and comforted by my church family. Still, I put on my happy face, dried up my tears, and thanked God that more importantly than having my name written favorably in Troy's journal, was to have my name written in the Lamb's Book of Life. Any hopes of building and strengthening our marriage through ministry in a foreign land were buried in the cemetery of failed attempts as our time in Taipei was drawing to a close. Yet I never stopped hoping and believing. By sowing seeds of kindness, I was bound to eventually reap a wonderful harvest.

37

World Tour 101

During our last few months in Taiwan, we started saving up our money to take a trip around the world before returning to the States. We invited Troy's brother Wayne and his wife, Terri, to join us, and we embarked on a four-month whirlwind world tour of Asia and Eastern Europe. Through the course of the summer, we walked on the Great Wall of China, toured the Taj Mahal, drank fermented mare's milk in Mongolia, rode a yak, enjoyed a scenic long-tailed boat ride through Bangkok, took a night train to Chang Mai, and explored silk factories and butterfly farms. We crossed the entire Soviet Union on the Trans-Siberian Railroad; visited temples that had been constructed even before Jesus walked on the earth; photographed the Himalayas shrouded in cloud cover at sunrise; toured winter palaces and summer palaces, gardens, mausoleums, castles, clock towers, the Hermitage, and Red Square with St. Basil's Cathedral. We filmed a dead man being cremated along a holy river, old yogis in caves on the hillside, and naked children swimming in the murky multipurpose river, where further upstream, women were washing their clothes. We mounted elephants and boarded rickety buses on narrow windy roads and flew on an airplane covered in smoke damage from a previous engine fire that kept us white-knuckled until we finally landed safely at our next destination. Having visited ten countries, we got a small sampling of a large part of the world, and the experience was incredible and life changing, to say the least.

Imagine how romantic to experience these sights and sounds with a lover. Picture yourselves snuggling up in the train car, trying to secretly make love in moments of privacy, sipping wine at an old cobblestone city square, holding hands, asking strangers to take pictures of you in front of the exotic monuments. Envision sitting on the beach, watching the sunset arm in arm or sharing a pastry in a funky little bakery. To see the world intertwined with a soul mate would make the adventure all the more magical. For five and a half years, Troy and I had been husband and wife, yet we had never been lovers. We had sex once every few months, but that barely constituted love. Even complete strangers could achieve the level of intimacy that we shared, with just an extra elixir or two at the bar. And for the entire four months, traveling, my heart longed for a taste of authentic affection and kindness, but it wasn't meant to be. The personalities of our group were in constant friction. One minute, Troy and Wayne would be at each other's throats competing for alpha male dominance. The next minute, they would be linking arms in solidarity as Wayne would scold Terri unmercifully or Troy would try to punish me for any perceived infraction. The reality was that our group consisted of three very strong-willed and opinionated travelers, each vying for control, and then there was me. I had been marginalized enough in my five years with Troy that I gladly deferred, taking a back seat to the daily decision-making. As a self-proclaimed peacemaker, my job was to simply follow my traveling companions around like a loyal retriever with tail wagging and tongue hanging out and listen for my commands to sit, stay, fetch, or come. It was all I believed I deserved.

I did, however, have one special request. I had purchased a video camera a year prior in Hong Kong and had spent multiple hours practicing using it for such a time as this. Because the others didn't want the extra bulk in their luggage and because I had the steadiest hand, I asked if I could be the primary videographer. I certainly didn't think it was too much to ask, considering I had virtually no say in anything else. Everyone seemed fine with the idea and agreed to then share the Olympus and Pentax amongst the three of them for the still shots. It was also understood that anyone was welcome to film if they wanted to, but I was the one responsible for keeping the batteries charged, the lens cleaned, and for the ongoing editing as we went along. My goal was to make the best compilation video I could as a fun keepsake—something we would want to watch and even show others without fear of them wanting to kill themselves from boredom. It truly seemed like a win-win situation. Even in the retelling, I find myself justifying why I *should've* been able to have control of my own camera. It speaks to the profound unworthiness I felt then and still feel even now, to have an opinion, to exercise a right to do something I want, or to have control over any aspect of my life. Troy called the shots. Troy told me what to do and how to think. This was a big move to let me take charge of the camera.

One night in Katmandu, I was out on the rooftop of our little guesthouse, looking at the stars and filming the spectacular view. I asked Troy if he would mind recording me with my new souvenir "Democracy" shirt that I was wearing. He said, "Yes, I would mind." At first I thought he was joking, but I noticed he wasn't smiling, and so I asked what he meant. He responded, rudely, "I have more important things to do than film you, like spending time with Wayne and Terri." *More important things to do.* The message I heard over and over through the years, like a dripping faucet: "I'm not important *enough,* lovable *enough,* worthy *enough.* I'm not *enough.* I'm *less than.* He couldn't take literally thirty seconds out of his day to point a camcorder at me and push the Record button because he had *more important things to do.* He continued, "That's what you get for being selfish with the camera." Taken aback, I asked, "What are you talking about?" He elaborated, "I'm not going to film you because you don't deserve to be in the video! Everyone thinks you are hogging the camera." I was confused. "I thought we all agreed that I would be in charge of the camcorder," I said. "How is that being selfish?" He said, "You think you are better than everyone else! That's why you erased a bunch of Wayne's footage, because it didn't meet your high and mighty expectations."

"Well, yeah, of course I deleted footage. I was editing!" I retorted defensively. Wayne had filmed fifteen minutes of footage in India out of the taxi window. We had four months of experiences to

capture, and I wanted to keep the scenes short. I edited my own filming constantly to make room on the camcorder tapes. It was nothing personal. But because I had cut some of his brother's footage, I
was no longer deemed worthy of being included, and just like that,
my presence was expunged from the record, cleaned and sanitized of
any evidence that I too had shared this magnificent adventure. This
was demoralizing beyond words, and I was completely crushed. The
thought of Troy, Wayne, and Terri talking behind my back was also
more than I could bear. Even if the allegations were true and I was
being possessive, the fact remained that it was my camera that I had
purchased with my own money. And it was my project, like a work
of art, that I was producing. Sharing the camera was like working
on an original painting and having others take the brush out of my
hand, whenever they wanted, to add their own details. So to freely
relinquish control when asked and yet still be judged as selfish added
insult to the injury. Feeling misunderstood and deeply hurt, I followed Troy down to the room and told him that I was going to give
the camcorder to Wayne and Terri to manage because I couldn't bear
going through the trip being criticized in this way. Troy was enraged.
"Oh no, you're not!" he screamed. "No one else is going to touch
it because you've made the video camera *your* god!" He yanked the
camera out of my hands, threw it on the bed, causing the viewfinder
to snap off, then shoved me on the bed, pinning me down as he
continued to scream vehemently at me. I fought and kicked, trying
to get him off me and threatened to bite him if he didn't let go. He
picked up the camera and assaulted me with it, slamming it into my
elbow as I tried to deflect the blow. When he let go for a second,
I cowered over to the corner of the bed. He followed me over and
started stuffing his fist in my mouth. "Bite me! *Bite me!* Go ahead!"
he screamed. "*Bite me!* That's what you want to do!" We had been
so careful to not push buttons in order to maintain a constant state
of copious indifference and a superficial peace, but years of pent-up
frustration were unexpectedly unleashed right then and there at Ben's
guesthouse on the other side of the world. I'm still a bit embarrassed
to this day that we represented our country so poorly, as we shared

our epic meltdown with the entire hotel. For the first time in our five years of marriage, I called him an asshole, and he was furious.

"Don't you *ever, ever* use language like that in front of me. Do you understand?" he scolded, as if talking to a rebellious teen. Never mind that he had called me a bitch more times than I could count.

He stormed out and headed toward Wayne and Terri's room to inform them that they weren't "allowed" to touch the camera and that *only* I could film for the rest of the trip. I yelled, "You are the biggest fucking asshole I've ever met! And I will say *fuck* if I want to!" I never hated him more than I did that night, and I simply dreaded the thought that I still had three and a half months to travel with this cruel, calculated, over-controlling, vindictive prick. I felt utterly broken and robbed of my remaining shred of self-worth. As if my life couldn't get any worse, that night, while sobbing mournfully in my pillow, I fell horribly ill. I had drunk bottled water in the village earlier, and when I got to my last few sips, I looked at the bottom of the bottle to discover green mossy fungus lining the inside of the plastic. I suspect that was the culprit as my body was burning up with fever, trying to kill whatever foreign bug I had ingested. I started vomiting and cramping up with diarrhea, while Troy lay still and unmoved, with his back toward me. My head throbbed. My entire body ached, alternating between burning up and shivering uncontrollably. Even the touch of the sheet hurt my skin. I showered with cold water and then lay on a wet towel, which kept drying from the body heat and needed to be redampened multiple times. Still Troy remained unresponsive with his back toward me despite the unmistakable echoes of heaving noises reverberating off the walls. My lips were parched, and I desperately needed water. I would've given anything to have my mom there, stroking my hair and assuring me everything would be all right. But I had absolutely no one. Emotionally, I was a wreck, and now physically, my body was following suit. I was literally too sick and weak to try and find water, and yet it was the only thing that could bring me any comfort. I could barely walk to the toilet without doubling over in pain, and feeling dizzy, let alone through the dark corridors of the hotel. I needed help. After suffering through the worst fight of the trip and literally weeping uncontrollably, from a place of complete despair, I now needed to ask Troy, my oppressor, to please find me some water. If he wouldn't even grant my simple request of taking my picture because *he had more important things to do*, how would he react if I asked him to get up in the middle of the night and wander around the premises in search of either boiled or bottled water, when just hours before, he had hit me, shoved me, pinned me down, screamed in my face, and tried to stuff his fist in my mouth? I had no choice. I woke him up and timidly asked for his help. Troy gave a long, exasperated sigh, got out of bed, slammed the door, and left without saying a word. The tremendous guilt engulfing me for imposing was temporarily overshadowed by quiet desperation. About ten to fifteen minutes later, he came back, handed me the water, and plopped back into bed and resumed his position, with back toward me. I gratefully thanked him, but he didn't respond. I didn't expect him to.

"You're welcome" would've implied that somehow I had deserved his kindness.

I had been wearing my Pollyanna lenses long enough to know that there was good in virtually every situation, even this one. I just needed to look beyond the vomit, diarrhea, fever, heartache, loneliness, anger, and grief to find the cup still half full. And there it was, lurking behind the scenes, waiting for me to notice. In my fundamental Christian world, where everything had a purpose and a lesson to be learned, the story unfolding in my head was this: God didn't want us to let the sun go down on our anger, so he allowed me to get sick so I would have to humble myself and ask Troy for help. And God didn't want Troy to simply go to sleep, leaving me alone and hurting, so he created a context by which Troy would "have" to reach out to me and serve me in some way. It wasn't perfect, but it was the best story I could come up with to make such a devastating ordeal have any redeeming merit. We woke up the next day and never spoke another word about it. We simply moved on as if the worst night of my life had been but a nightmare, which was vanquished at the first signs of morning light.

The following is an excerpt from my journal entry a few weeks later.

> Journal
> July 18, 1990
> (Soviet Union)
>
> It seems a shame that if we claim to have Jesus Christ ruling our lives and uniting our hearts, we have nothing to show for it. I wish we could be a model couple with a marriage that people admire instead of one that people despise.
>
> I told Troy I was miserable and wondered why he even married me. I asked him to please level with me and let me know where I stood with him. He said, "If I told you how I felt about you, you'd kill yourself."

Well, thank goodness he spared my feelings! A healthier person would've left him, but I couldn't. I was a battered woman, looking through the distorted lens of faith and not reality. My Bible assured me that despite how crazy and dysfunctional everything seemed on the surface, somehow it was all still a part of God's plan. Who was I to tell the potter how to form his clay? What God had joined together, let no man put asunder. God was still working through us. He wasn't finished yet, and I just needed to be patient.

We had started our grand adventure in May, and in August, we set foot on American soil for the first time since we had left for Taiwan, two years prior.

I looked back on our World 101 tour with profound gratitude that I had seen and done so much. I didn't want the relational trauma to taint my memory of such an amazing experience. I reminded myself that it could've been worse. We could've been mugged, killed, injured, or kidnapped. We could've picked up a deadly disease or lost our passports. Any number of things *could've* gone wrong, but they didn't. Instead we made it safely back to the States with forty-eight rolls of film, ten camcorder tapes chronicling everyone but me, good health, and experiences to draw strength from for the rest of our lives. As broken and wounded as I was in spirit, somehow I was still able to find the good in my circumstances and keep that contented smile firmly planted on my countenance. In the big scheme of things, my cup was more than half full. It was overflowing, and as always, I gave all the thanks and glory to my creator and sustainer. I concluded, "How would I have *ever* survived without Jesus?"

38

Take Me Home, Country Road

We had left our sporty red Mazda Rx7 at Troy's parents' place when we moved to Taiwan, and so our first stop was in Montana to pick up the car and begin our long road trip back to California. With close to six years of marriage under our belt, we had lived in a foreign country, learned to speak Mandarin, traveled the world, fulfilled a lifetime's worth of bucket lists, and discovered a myriad of different cultures and customs, with sights, sounds, and smells that often offended our senses. Hopefully, we were older and wiser, more seasoned for this next chapter, and perhaps we could draw from our reservoir of "hard knocks" to help us navigate more maturely this next time around. So with all the hope and optimism of Easter morn and the promise of new life and do-overs, I buckled up my seatbelt and joyfully embraced the journey home. Slowly, we waved good-bye to Troy's parents, started driving down the gravel road to the mailbox, turned right, and we were off. Troy said, "Get the little notebook from the glove compartment and record the number on the odometer so we can keep track of gas mileage on the trip home." I immediately did as I was instructed, but I needed just a second to think through the formula because it had been two years since I had made an entry on the ledger. "Here, give it to me," Troy impatiently demanded. I didn't need or want his help, and so I said, "No, that's okay. I've got it." Again, he demanded, with more force, "I said, *give me the book*, Joy!" *Oh brother! Here we go again.* Two minutes out the door, and it's a déjà vu of our road trip from five years ago. Nothing had changed. Had we not learned a goddamned thing in five years? I simply couldn't tolerate being bullied even a second longer. I said, "Troy, I am perfectly capable of doing this. I want to do it, and I don't want you treating me like I'm too retarded to figure it out." I had pushed a button that couldn't be retracted, and Troy was instantaneously trembling with rage. How dare I not give him the mileage log! He reached over, snatched it out of my hand, and threw it out the window into the ditch, where it vanished into the dense, waist-deep brush. Then once again, in his old, familiar way, with blood vessels bulging and face beet-red, he responded, "There! Are you happy now? The book is gone, so you can just stop your whining!"

Oh, how I wanted to show him just once what real whining sounded like, but this wasn't the time. Instead I said, "What the heck, Troy! Why did you do that? Just stop the car and I'll go find it." I flinched, half expecting him to hit me for talking back, but instead, he floored the gas and drove the car right into the ditch, blowing out a tire, destroying the axle and thrashing the alignment. We were literally three-fourths of a mile from the ranch. That's as far as we got before Troy started his tantrum and derailed our plans right out of the gate. I wanted so badly to walk back to the ranch and tell Troy's parents what he had just done, but of course, I couldn't. I felt just like the tire, only a second ago filled to the brim with air, aligned, and ready to make the journey, and without warning, suddenly deflated and broken, stuck in the ditch and reduced to useless rubble. It took literally a full extra day to get the car drivable and several hundred dollars that we were counting on to resettle in California. I was tired of rationalizing Troy's toxic behavior. I wondered if this was going to be my life. What if Troy didn't change? What then? I needed a different perspective. I needed to see the situation from God's vantage point. Before I could even consult God on the matter, I knew I was not going to get any comfort from Him. I wanted to put my fingers in my ears and sing "lalalalala" to drown the voice indicting me. I knew, in my heart of hearts, I should've just submitted and handed over the notebook. That's what good wives do. That's what godly wives do. But I didn't want to and couldn't even will myself to surrender. After all these years of asking the Holy Spirit to help me "want" to yield to his bossy demands, I still resented it as much as I did five years prior. Why couldn't I get it through my thick head? I wrestled internally with this "revelation" because it felt like an ongoing death blow to my own personhood. I cried out to God, begging him to change my wicked, proud, stubborn heart, and I resolved to do better. Still, I couldn't bring myself to apologize, and like every other conflict, we quietly picked up the shattered pieces and carried on as if nothing had happened.

When we finally made it to Pasadena, I couldn't wait to go back to Abundant Life, my sanctuary, my refuge, my "*other* husband." When we entered church the following Sunday, I ran down the aisle, with my hands extended to heaven, laughing and crying as the beautiful music was playing through the speakers, and I thanked God, from the deep wellspring of my heart, for bringing me home. I embraced my caring friends with all the emotion and tenderness of a soldier returning from war. I felt safe and loved. I was once again in the nurturing arms of Jesus.

39

Marriage Retreat

Shortly after returning to Pasadena, we signed up for our first ever Christian marriage retreat. "Unless you are intentionally moving together, your natural tendency will always be to drift," the pastor warned. He encouraged us to identify areas of drifting in our marriages and to ask God to help us move together. At the end of the session, we were assigned to go to our rooms and rate our relationship on a scale of 1 to 10, 1 being the worst and 10 being the best. I had never allowed myself to evaluate my marriage honestly. For six years, I sought to find the cup half full or the spiritual lessons to be learned. I couldn't just admit that my marriage was a train wreck. Such an assessment would imply that I wasn't grateful for what God was trying to show me or teach me. Every hardship was God-ordained, so I had no right to complain or bemoan my struggles. But that night, I tried to answer from my gut and not from my "faith" script. From my perspective, we had grown so far apart that we didn't even register on the grid. I gave us a rating of "minus 2." Troy seemed taken aback that I had felt this way. Perhaps it was because I had been so careful to hide my feelings and needs over the years that I gave the impression things were better than they were. He, on the other hand, awarded us a generous 4. We met in small groups the next day to share our results with other couples. I was coming down with pink eye, one of the fallouts of teaching first grade in a public school, and my eyes were goopy and watering, giving the appearance that I was terribly distraught. The church leaders were alerted, and before I knew it, my puffy eyes along with my negative marriage score were prompting an emergency intervention. We were encouraged to get into counseling immediately. Students in the Fuller Seminary marriage and family program needed clients to practice on, and so we became their guinea pigs for a reduced fee. After a few sessions, the counselor felt that a season of individual meetings with Troy would be more beneficial because he had some "personal" issues to work through. Troy stuffed down his feelings like a vacuum-sealed sweater bag, refusing to share his emotions with me, despite my pleas for him to open up. It was only when the pressure became too great that he would explode, and rage became the one emotion I was allowed to see. So it was a tremendous relief that he had a safe place to vent.

During that time, our marriage began to improve a bit, and we even talked about starting a family. With my biological clock ticking at an amplified decibel, motherhood trumped all other desires and aspirations. Our seven years of heartache would be worth it for the joy of creating a child together to raise up in the fear of the Lord. Our previous failed attempts at marital bliss through ministry and travel left us disillusioned, but we were both optimistic that this next venture into parenthood would keep the marriage knot secured.

40

Parenthood!

My wish came true, when our first daughter, Mackenzie Joy, was forcibly plucked from my uterus with a suction cup on her head and a nurse pushing on my stomach. The corners of her tiny mouth turned up in a perpetual smile, and her little cry sounded like a bleating lamb. Every grand adventure that had once topped my list of experiences now paled in comparison to holding my own tender, breathtaking offspring in my arms. When I lay eyes on Mackenzie and pulled her to my breast to nurse, my heart was bursting. This "too awesome to be named" emotion was unlike anything I had ever experienced. It poured down my cheeks, escaped from my lips, channeled through my caressing fingers, permeated every fiber in my being, filled up my soul to overflowing. It turned my mourning into dancing and flooded my emotions with indescribable bliss. I felt like I was experiencing the purest and most authentic love for the very first time, so deep and profound I would never be able to exhaust its abundant reservoir. The birth of my daughter erased the endless aching and longing of my injured heart. I was alive and whole and grateful beyond words to have been given the desire expressed so many times through muffled sobs. I couldn't stop thanking and praising God for this most remarkable and special gift.

Troy, to my delight, was a devoted dad, incredibly attentive, protective, and nurturing. He even helped change diapers without gagging, a level of sainthood that other godly men hadn't yet achieved. I saw a gentle side of him that had never been visible before. Having a baby in the house took the focus off our tumultuous relationship and projected it onto our helpless, needy offspring. The one thing we both shared was our adoration for the precious baby we had made together. She filled a void in each of us and gave life new meaning. And as the old adage goes, if one is good, two must be better, right? And so we had four within four years! Our firstborn became a big sister to two more girls, Savannah and Sterling, and a baby brother, Dakota. A few years later, we would even up the gender score by adopting two more treasures, giving us six kids to make our family complete and our love cup full.

41

Doesn't Play Well with Others

I wish I could say that becoming a parent changed Troy's DNA somehow and his cruel narcissism fell by the wayside, but unfortunately it didn't. He couldn't change his personality any more than a zebra could change his stripes, despite the "indwelling Holy Spirit" supposedly sanctifying him.

Troy had wanted to be in the ministry since he was a teenager, when he believed he had received his divine call. His prestigious MDiv from Fuller Seminary should have given him a shoe in, but his abrasive nature kept getting in the way. No matter how hard he tried, he simply was incapable of treating others with the kindness and respect befitting of a pastor. He seemed to have no filter and said and did whatever came to mind, without any consideration of people's feelings. If he insulted, demoralized, or frightened those he encountered, including small vulnerable children, he claimed it was their fault or their problem for just being too sensitive. He would come home from work complaining how stupid and pathetic the women in his office were because something he had said made them cry. One time, his sister was having a birthday but made it clear she wanted no baby gifts even though she had just announced that she was pregnant. Troy bought a pacifier anyway, and when she refused it, he angrily shoved it down her blouse. When Troy's brother and girlfriend came to visit, shortly after we first moved to California and were apartment managers, he hid behind a wall to catch the girl sneaking over to Wayne's room. When he saw her, he jumped out and literally pinned her against the wall, with clumps of her blouse wadded in his fist, and demanded, "*Get back to your own room!* I've already warned you not to sleep with my brother! What part of this arrangement are you too stupid to understand?" That was the last we saw of Katie as she announced, "This is the most fucked-up family I've ever seen!" He terrified his students in Sunday school with his strict, authoritarian approach and frightened the neighbor kids by literally chasing them off our property while screaming at them as they fled in panic. One little girl fell in a prickly rose bush trying to escape, and her father came knocking on our door, completely dumbfounded that a grown man would so brutally terrorize a five-year-old for playing in our tree. Hitler was the nickname assigned him at the public high school where he subbed for a short season, before cracking under the stress of not being able to control the rowdy teens. Even many of my friends didn't want to come around when he was home because they were intimidated. Somehow, though, he never could pick up clues that his actions were socially unacceptable. Unless someone pointed it out to him that he was being too harsh, he wouldn't know it. And even if he adjusted his behavior in one situation, he couldn't seem to transfer the protocol to another setting. I found myself constantly apologizing on his behalf because I felt his actions were reflecting on me, as his spouse. "He didn't mean to come across that way." "His bark is worse than his bite." "He sounds rude, but his intentions are good." With lots of coaching, he showed signs of improvement, and I was beginning to feel like maybe the worst was over and we were moving closer toward normalcy. But just when I would let my guard down and start to trust that I was safe, his impulsivity would resurface, catching me off guard. When Mackenzie was a baby, I remember holding her as we got into a heated argument over purchasing a $15 whiteboard that I needed to do math tutoring. I should have accepted his immediate "no," but I felt the need to explain that the money could be recovered by just a couple of tutoring sessions. Disagreeing with him, however, was unacceptable, and before I knew it, he was trying to take the baby from me as leverage and threatening to leave with her, claiming I was unfit to be a mother. He knew exactly what buttons to push to regain control, and attacking my motherhood was a cheap shot that immediately did the trick. Terrified, I started kicking him away, and he grabbed my leg, causing me to fall to the ground as he ripped Mackenzie from my arms amidst my screaming and pleading to give her back. It wasn't until I started to call the police that he relented, before storming out of the house and disappearing until later that night. I went to my best friend Marni's house, who lived only a mile away, completely distraught and sharing with her what had happened along with other prior incidents, which had followed a similar pattern. "Joy, you are in an abusive relationship and you are not safe!" she pleaded. "Call the pastors and make an appointment for counseling, but in the meantime, you should not go home." She advised me to check in to a women's shelter close by, but the thought was inconceivable. Perhaps she had misunderstood me. I wasn't being abused. Troy was a jerk and had threatened to kidnap our child over a $15 whiteboard, but I wasn't being beat up. In my mind, we had just gotten into a fight that got out of hand. It was merely one of many isolated incidents, and everything would be fine. In hindsight, I realize that Marni had been my only true advocate, seeing the situation for what it was, but I couldn't receive help because my brain was conditioned to gloss over and excuse Troy's behavior. Consequently, my only life rope I latched onto was the church, which kept me locked into a dysfunctional cycle of patriarchal control.

42

Train up a Child

Sadly, as the children grew older, much of the violence that had once been directed toward others and myself was transferred to the children during discipline. His intimidation weapon was to pull his belt off his pants and slam it viciously against his desk to scare them, as papers would fly off and coffee mugs would crash to the ground in a thousand pieces. He would also poke them repeatedly in the chest and pull their ears while shouting, "What's wrong with your ears? Can't they hear? Are they deaf? Is that why you can't follow directions?" Putting his hand over their mouth to make them stop wailing after getting a severe spanking was evocative of how he treated me in the early years when he wanted me to shut up. When they were disobedient, he accused them of hating God and insisted, much to their pleading rebuttals, that they were thinking God was a stupid idiot and they didn't have to listen to Him. This was another example of his assumptions being projected as fact and claiming to know what they were thinking, when, in fact, he didn't. As much as I tried to love and respect Troy, I couldn't help but feel repulsed when he treated the children with such aggression. Everything in me wanted to recoil in anger and disgust, and yet, to be a submissive and godly wife, I couldn't pull away.

When Troy wasn't putting the fear of God into the kids, he was attentive, and the children aspired to please him. He read to them every night before they went to bed and helped them memorize Westminster's shorter catechism. One morning in Sunday school, a new child in our son's preschool class asked, "Who's God?" and our four-year-old stood up and announced, "Dod is a thpirit whose being, power, wisdom, holiness, justice, doodness, and troof are infinite, eternal, and unchangeable." Then he sat down and resumed his coloring/scribbling outside the lines, as his teacher stood, mouth gaping, in reverent awe of Troy's unsurpassed spiritual training of his kids.

But there is a fine line between training and controlling, and the lines were often blurred as Troy sought to micromanage every detail of the children's lives. What people also didn't see behind the scenes were horror stories of control turning into abuse. When our daughter Savannah was a toddler, she was standing next to Troy, holding on to his leg. She bent down and put her mouth on his knee, like little kids sometimes do, as they explore with their senses. Then without warning, her "taste" became a bite, and Troy swiftly and aggressively grabbed her onto his lap to scold her severely. He frightened her so badly that she started to wet her pants.

"You just peed on me! You did that on purpose!" Troy screamed. He instantly turned her over his knee and started spanking her violently, as I watched in horror trying to calm him down and explain that she was just a baby. There were countless instances where he punished the kids simply for being immature children. For example, the cousins were visiting for the very first time from out of state, which was special and a huge deal. The kids were going to watch a movie before bedtime, and our six-year-old had been anticipating this moment all day. In her excitement, she carelessly sat on the VHS box. Troy reprimanded her severely, as if she had deliberately mishandled the plastic case. Before she had a chance to move it to a safe location, she accidentally sat on it again. She immediately realized what she had done and begged her daddy to forgive her, but it was too late. Troy immediately banished her to her room, where her heartbroken sobs echoed through the house as she lay in her bed, crushed from being ostracized and publicly humiliated in front of her cousins.

One time, he went along with us to the Science Center on a homeschooling field trip. I remember leaving the exhibit hall to take one of the kids to the bathroom. When I was heading back to find the family, I could hear a man yelling very loudly. My heart nearly stopped, and I was immediately flooded with fear as I recognized Troy's voice. Standing in a crowd of dozens or more of mommies and children, he chose to berate one of our children so loudly that he could be heard in the next room. I raced over as quickly as I could, begging him to please lower his voice. He refused, saying that the child deserved the correction. I wanted so badly to snatch our kids away to a safe corner and just hold them and cry, but I couldn't. Troy was in charge and I wasn't.

When the youngest was four, we took a trip to Ohio to film a children's program that we wanted to pitch to PBS. We were staying at some friends' house, and all four kids were sleeping on the floor of our bedroom. With a four-, five-, six-, and eight-year-old in one room, it's not hard to imagine that they might giggle and play and not fall asleep on cue. One night, Troy heard them playing and flew into a rage. He stormed in, pulling up one daughter off the floor by her head because she wasn't "looking at him" when he was scolding her and proceeded to scream at her to go to sleep. He picked up the youngest one and literally dropped him on the ground, demanding that he lie down and stay down. I was trembling with fear, as were the poor, helpless victims of his temper.

Yosemite was another vacation that should be remembered for the beautiful hikes, climbing Half Dome, and nightly campfires. But the story that is burned in my memory is of one child being banished to the Suburban alone in the pouring rain for literally hours because she had been unkind to her little sister. The hurt and despair in her eyes as the family was told they could not talk or interact with her left me aching and confused. Everything in me screamed to rescue her, hold her, hug her, reassure her that she was deeply loved. Had I not feared the repercussions, I would've screamed obscenities at Troy for being so cruel and insensitive and so emotionally abusive. But I could do neither. Instead, I sat powerless and stripped of any agency to act.

It didn't help that Abundant Life, our spiritual safe house, was going through some significant changes of its own, both in leadership as well as theology. Our free-flowing, spirit-filled meetings were becoming more authoritarian, and the grace messages were being replaced with an entire year-long series on sin. We were told that unless we fully understood our utter depravity, we would never be able to appreciate the gospel. The Puritan fathers were the only theologians quoted from the pulpit because they had a clear understanding of God's fiery wrath and our need to pursue holiness.

This heavy emphasis on sin permeated into child-rearing as well. Our job as Christian parents was to unapologetically insist on complete obedience from our children, at all times. They were instructed to "obey right away, all the way, and in the right way" or they would be chastised with the "rod of correction." By teaching them to submit to our authority, we were helping them to eventually submit to God. At one of the church-sponsored parenting seminars, the pastor asked the sound technician to turn off the recording device while he instructed us to literally beat our children. He said it was okay to leave marks and welts. The important thing was that we were to give as many smacks as needed until we had broken their will and their cry of defiance had turned to cries of repentance. The pastor confessed that he had once spent three hours disciplining his young son until he got the cry of surrender he was looking for!

I wasn't against spanking, as a general rule. In fact, I believed pain was not evil or immoral. It was actually a built-in life-saving mechanism. Without the sensation of pain, we could touch a burning stove and not realize we needed to move our hand away until it was too late. And so I could see how a sting on the backside could help extinguish undesirable behavior. This instruction, however, was way more than what I was comfortable with, and alarms were going off in my head, warning me, "This isn't right!" Yet we were told that we were harming our children *more* by not taking sin seriously and punishing our kids as their sins deserved. As a teacher, I could handle thirty first graders for six hours a day without ever resorting to corporal punishment, and so I naturally used many of the basic classroom management skills at home, limiting the use of spanking to extreme situations. But Troy took his role of biblical dad quite seriously and never missed an opportunity to "drive away foolishness with a good paddling." And even though I couldn't do it personally, I delivered the kids right into his hands as a willing accomplice to the physical trauma and emotional scarring. This heavy-handed discipline had a way of ruining virtually every vacation and family outing, as Troy had to mete out consequences for the tiniest of infractions. My stomach was in knots constantly as I watched the children cower in fear.

And yet my special glasses offered a hint of superficial comfort. "Train up a child in the way that he shall go, and when he is old, he will not depart from it." My entire life as a Christian was counterintuitive. Whatever felt right was obviously wrong. And whatever was uncomfortable, unpleasant, or humbling was usually right. Taking the narrow road, the one less traveled, while painful, would lead our children to eternal life, so I tried to snuff out my protective instincts as I deferred to my husband and to God.

43

Hostage Crisis

The only educational path for my children that was truly sanctioned by the church was homeschooling, which I embraced fully. Wearing my denim jumper, accessorized by a cross necklace and thick sandals or Keds on my feet (the unspoken Christian "uniform" of the homeschool community), I blended in nicely with the other thousands of moms at the annual Home School Legal Defense Association (HSLDA) convention each year. Like the others, I was committed to raising up the next generation to read, write, think, and speak from a biblical worldview.

Our carefree homeschooling groove became interrupted when Troy decided to telecommute rather than work in an office fifteen minutes away. While ideal for him, since he didn't have to carpool to work, it was less than desirable for the rest of us. For one, our house was only seven hundred square feet, and with Troy taking up one of the rooms all day, it became smaller still. It no longer was a place where the kids could run around, play, sing songs, make noise, or watch PBS during their down time. Because his office was directly in the center of the house, surrounded by the bedrooms, kitchen, and living room, everything we did reverberated off the thin walls, affecting his ability to make phone calls, which was 90 percent of his job description as an insurance adjuster. It was as if our house had become his office and we were confined to the waiting room with quiet feet and inside voices. Thankfully, we lived in Southern California and the little ones could play outside. We had also converted the garage into a makeshift school room, so we did most of our lessons out there, but it was often damp and cold and terribly inconvenient to not have full access to our living space, especially with a three-, four-, five-, and seven-year-old in tow. There was no benefit for us to have Troy home because we had to adjust our routine for him, but he was unwilling to make any accommodations for us. He made it clear that even though he was home, he would never help with the kids during working hours. I needed to just pretend he wasn't there. It would've been fine if the rules applied to everyone. But his friends from church could come by at any time without calling first, and he would immediately stop what he was doing and hang out over a cup of coffee. And he, personally, could come and go as he pleased without adhering to a rigid schedule. In other words, the restrictions only applied to me.

Things came to a head, though, one fateful day, when I thought it would be okay to leave the seven-year-old at home for fifteen minutes to complete her math lesson, while I dropped off one of the siblings at her co-op. I wasn't asking Troy to babysit. Mackenzie was perfectly capable of working independently while I was gone and obviously posed no danger to herself. I just wanted her to keep working so she would be finished in time for her co-op classes later. I knocked on his door, popped my head in and informed Troy, more as a courtesy, than anything, that Mackenzie was in the school room working and I would be right back. I assured him that I didn't need him to do anything but just wanted him to know. He stopped typing and scowled. "I thought it was understood that I'm not watching the kids during working hours." "I get that, but I'm not asking you to watch her," I said. At that point, I recognized an argument about to ensue, and so I backpedaled. "Never mind," I said, and I headed to the garage to get Mackenzie and tell her to join her siblings in the car. When I came back through the house, Troy, visibly angry, stopped me. "We are not done with this conversation!" he demanded. I told him we could discuss it later because I needed to get Savannah to her class. He said, "You are not going anywhere because I just said the conversation isn't over." Suddenly his work could wait.

"Troy, there's nothing more to be said," I responded. "My intention wasn't to ask you to babysit, but I understand your perspective and I won't do it again."

"No, that's not true. You ob-vious-ly [stretching out every syllable] think you are in the right, and so yes, we do have more to talk about!"

"Troy, I don't want to argue with you and I don't have time to justify my actions." With that, I ran out the door and jumped into the minivan.

"Get back in the house!" he angrily demanded, from the front steps, as we were all getting buckled up in the car. Quickly I locked the doors and started the engine. I just shook my head and mouthed the words "Sorry, I have to go." Suddenly he lunged for the car and began banging at the rear of the vehicle as if he were trying to break the window. All four kids, terrified, started crying in unison. I put the gear in reverse and released the brake slowly, as a warning for him to get out of the way. He slammed his fist on the window one more time as hard as he could, accusing me of trying to run him over, before stepping aside, and stared at me with a look of such hatred that I could feel the color drain from my face. I headed toward the co-op literally shaking as I tried to comfort the crying kids, who were asking why Daddy was so mad. I was terrified to go home because I had disobeyed my husband and I knew I was in big trouble. I drove around while waiting for the kids' class to end, trying to think through my options. When we got home, Troy was waiting for me at the door and barked, "You, go sit on the couch!"

"Kids, I need you to go outside and play while Mommy and Daddy talk. Don't come back inside until I come and get you, okay?" I said. I'll never forget the trepidation on their faces as they obediently started to walk away.

"The kids aren't going anywhere. Get back here and sit down!" Troy ordered. They immediately ran to me for comfort and in a way to offer their solidarity. The three-year-old crawled in my lap as the other little ones latched onto each arm.

"You don't need to sit by Mom," Troy scolded. Instead, he demanded they take a spot on the floor, as a control tactic, not only to make me feel isolated and alone but to rob them of any sense of comfort as well. He barked his orders with the same intensity and authority as a bank robber instructing his hostages. On cue, they all burst into loud sobbing, holding their hands out to me to rescue them as Troy yanked them from my grip and plopped them down on the area rug, out of reach.

"Please, just let them go outside!" I pleaded. "They don't need to see us arguing. Look how terrified they are. Please don't do this."

"I can do whatever I want to do because I'm the dad. Do you understand? Can you understand that? Can you get that through your head?"

Troy forced the kids to stop crying by threatening to spank them if they didn't calm down. Still, their little lips quivered as they tried to steady their breathing. When he had the children where he wanted them, he finally said, "Now, we are going to have the conversation, and you are *not* going to leave until I say we are done!" Then he proceeded to accuse me, as he had done before, of being an unfit mother, claiming that I was as bad as the drug dealer neighbor next door who let her two-year-old run in the street unattended. He knew what he was doing. This line of attack was intentional and cruel, designed to break me and gain the upper hand. Blindsided, I fell into his manipulative trap. He could criticize my house cleaning skills or my habit of leaving cupboard doors ajar or even my inability to put his dress shirts on the hanger with the precision he demanded. But to attack my motherhood, the one thing that meant more to me than life itself, the job into which I tirelessly and willingly poured myself and the title I held with such deep and holy reverence, was a blow too devastating to remain confined in the hidden chambers of my heart. I wanted to release it through my lungs with a deafening and piercing primordial scream that would alert the world, what I was feeling. But instead, I tried to reason with him. I repeated over and over that while I disagreed with his assessment of me, I understood his point of view and promised not do it again. Each time he responded, "No, you obviously don't understand! If you understood, you wouldn't have done it."

Once again, he ignored and dismissed my words as irrelevant because his assumptions held more weight. It simply wasn't okay for me to share a different perspective. Until I agreed that he was right and I was wrong, I was not going to be let off the couch. But no matter what I said, he insisted I didn't get it and that I wasn't repentant enough. This went on and on until I was emotionally exhausted. I just wanted the nightmare to end, and so I started to get up and he shoved me back on the couch. Towering over me like a white Protestant slave master breaking in his newly owned merchandise, he warned, "*You* are not leaving until I say you can leave! Now *sit. Back. Down!*"

Even writing this now brings back so much pain that my primordial scream is still brewing, waiting to erupt with all the fury of Mount St. Helens. In desperation, I sobbed, "I don't know what else I can say or do. You've made me feel so worthless and unlovable I just want to die. I can't do this. I've learned my lesson. I've promised not to ask for help while you are working. What else do you want from me? Do you need to hit me to teach me a lesson? Whatever it takes, just do it right now! But I can't continue this anymore." By this time, I was hysterical and weeping. I remember even pulling my own hair and slapping myself, trying to gain his forgiveness, but he wouldn't let me go until he knew he had completely broken me.

Like so many other traumatic encounters, my memory has blocked out some of the details and I don't know how the standoff ended. But at some point, I recall seeing our pastor later that day as he was picking up his kids from the church co-op, and he asked me how I was doing. Still trembling, I burst into tears as I shared with him what had happened and for the first time I felt that I had been heard. During pastoral counseling, I was still rebuked for not submitting, but this time, Troy wasn't let off the hook. That was the final nail in the coffin for any chance he would have to be a pastor within our group of churches.

When the elders told Troy that he just wasn't "pastor material" and asked him to step down from the internship he had been in to be evaluated and trained, Troy was devastated. It was the only thing he had ever truly wanted, and for the very first time, I saw him weep. He was broken and contrite but not over his own short-comings. He had trivialized my concerns as well as disregarded the evaluation of the pastors. He wasn't grieving the emotional harm he had brought to his family. He showed no remorse for holding the kids and I hostage. He was distraught because he felt he had been misunderstood and wrongly judged by the pastors. They were keeping him from fulfilling his lifelong, God-given calling. At this point, I was beginning to suspect that Troy was delusional. How could he not see that his actions were catastrophically damaging? He honestly believed that everyone else was the problem and he was the victim! Still, I believed, as I was taught, that every problem, big or small, was a spiritual matter and the solution could be found in the pages of scripture. He needed the Holy Spirit to open his eyes and cure his spiritual blindness. Meanwhile, my job was to simply forgive, let go of bitterness, and pray.

44

The Frog Prince

Despite chapters of painful remembrances, still raw in the retelling, there were happy moments as well that I latched onto as proof that God was still doing a good work in our marriage. My faith was bolstered even more when it appeared that Troy was having a "rebirth" of sorts. After fifteen years of keeping me at arm's length, as I followed longingly from a distance like a stray dog, hoping for an occasional scrap or pat on the head, Troy had received an epiphany. His counselor told him that the moment he said "I do," the marriage had become sacred and was indeed God's perfect will. So he encouraged Troy to reach out and love me as the bride God had chosen for him and to see our union as blessed by the Lord. For some reason, the pastor's words finally clicked, and Troy, after a decade and a half of bitter resistance, slowly started to warm up to me. His countenance was less gruff, and he even complimented me on occasion. When he told me he loved me, I was beginning to believe he actually meant it. He even initiated regular "date nights," something the more "spiritual" couples in church did to keep the marriage vows fresh. It didn't usually involve shallow carnal pleasures like movies, bowling, or shopping. Oh no. That would distract from the God talk. When you take the *fun* out of *fundie*, you get the word *die*. That's sometimes what it felt like, even though I knew we were heading in the right direction and tried my best to be thankful. Date nights for Christians were more like accountability checkups, where we shared what God was teaching us or what we were reading during our "quiet time." For several months, despite the fact I hate coffee, he took me to Starbucks while the kids went to their Bible club called AWANA. Watching him drink his coffee while I sipped my loathsome bottled water, a poor substitute for Diet Coke, my beverage of choice, not included on the menu, and sharing about our "aha" moments from the Bible was not what I considered a good time, and yet, I knew it was despicable of me to not to embrace the "miracle." Troy was transforming, and I needed to be on board. Looking back, I can admit that I dreaded these weekly encounters, but at the time, my feelings were completely divorced from my sense of obligation, and the uncomfortable knot in my stomach seemed as normal as indigestion after pizza. The church told me what I *should* feel, and when my experience was different, I just willed it to be so, erasing my real feelings and replacing them with the "right" ones. Thankful for the progress we were making as a couple, I washed down my ingratitude with my Aquafina and convinced myself that I was having a wonderful time, as any dutiful Christian wife *should.*

All those years of patience, perseverance, fasting, and prayer were coming to fruition. The testimony I always believed I would share one day, recounting God's faithfulness to resurrect our marriage from the ashes, was ready to be penned. My warty old frog was slowly turning into a prince. Yet our struggles were far from over. My fairy tale ending with "happily ever after" had to wait as I too was under a spell, trapped in a prison of brokenness and waiting for the magic kiss that would set me free.

45

Damaged Goods

It became obvious that the trauma over the years had taken its toll. One can't be reviled for years, without being emotionally and psychologically damaged. For the first fifteen years, I had slept on the far edge of the bed, just as I had been trained, and had kept a safe distance so as not to smother. For fifteen years, I saw myself as inferior, unworthy of intimacy, sexually repulsive, and incapable of being loved by any man. I remember watching romantic movies and having no schema to draw from to understand the loving and playful exchange. I had never felt it or experienced it, and I even tensed up when the lovers on screen would have sex. Why wasn't she fearful and cautious? Why wasn't she repulsed? How could she jump freely into his arms as he spun her around kissing her?

For fifteen years, I suppressed my desire for physical love and, instead, always sought to draw my attention and affection to Jesus. I had capped off every emotional pathway leading to intimacy as a protective coping mechanism. With emotions detached, Troy and I could function like roommates, sharing responsibilities, making decisions, and managing our home with very little fighting. Eventually the desire to love and be loved by Troy just withered and died. I continued to do all the things a good wife does, from a "to-do" list in my head and not from any heart connection. As a Christian, I had become an expert at overriding my feelings in order to follow Jesus. In the arena of faith, feelings seemed to just get in the way and were discounted regularly as menaces to truth. This way of relating to

Troy was working fine until Troy's miraculous awakening. He started moving closer to me in bed and even began putting his arm across my chest to snuggle. But I still hugged the far edge of the bed, only this time, not from habit; I no longer *wanted* to be touched or held by him. My brain, no matter how hard I prayed, would never register him as safe. Troy started initiating sex a lot more like once or twice a week, which should have been a welcome change but to me felt invasive and suffocating. I had lost my ability to feel arousal. That connection had weakened with each cruel blow and deliberate refusal to acknowledge my feelings and needs. And while I longed for him to make love to me over the years, it wasn't because I was turned on. It was because I couldn't bear the constant sting of rejection. I felt like a cold, dead engine, literally willing myself to engage. He was now giving me everything I had ever craved, but I simply couldn't reactivate the damaged receptors sending messages back and forth from the body to the brain, granting permission to feel. I prayed fervently that God would change my heart, but to no avail. So while Troy wanted to "make love," the only thing I could offer and receive was empty, hollow sex, because, without a strong, healthy, emotional bond, true intimacy isn't possible. I was committed to the process of dying to self and uprooting pride and thus couldn't give any credence to the internal struggles I was facing. I felt ashamed that I didn't have romantic feelings or that I felt repulsed and sometimes even angry when Troy would force my hand into foreplay. I couldn't admit that I wanted to recoil in self-protection and that being touched filled me with dread, even on special romantic getaways. In fact, any vacation that involved sex left me anxious and stressed rather than excited and renewed. But I knew, despite my aversion, I had to honor the marriage bed. It wasn't optional. I would have to just go into autopilot and make myself available against every instinct to retreat.

It's ironic that for the first half of my marriage, I had to endure the pain of desiring intimacy but not getting it, and in the second half, I was forced to endure the pain of intimacy without desire. I was so used to living in denial of my feelings, though, that the discomfort and numbness seemed normal. That's just what it's supposed to feel like when following Christ.

I accepted this arrangement as God's ultimate best. What else did I have to compare it to? The idea of enduring and persevering was hailed as more important than experiencing a dynamic, mutually satisfying connection. Without feelings, our only measurement of success was an external checklist, which we were good at following, in the same way we tallied our spiritual disciplines of Bible study and intercession. Did we have a date night? Check. Were we having sex regularly? Check. Were we faithful? Check. Did we kiss good night? Check. All I needed to do was keep my feelings deeply buried, force myself to go through the motions, praise God daily for the miraculous changes, repent for not wanting what God was graciously providing, and continue to beg God to change my heart. Check.

Because I had never experienced any relationship other than the one I was in, I didn't even know what was possible. So whenever people would ask how we were doing, I would automatically answer, "Great!" and I meant it. By all external measures, we were a decent couple—world travelers, setting foot on all seven continents, active in the community, raising a bunch of kids together, and beating the divorce odds. What could I possibly complain about? When people asked if I was happily married, again, I would give a resounding *yes*, not having a clue what real happiness should feel like. We were housemates who had learned to live together, and we functioned like a well-oiled machine. This, in my mind, was as good as it would ever get and I had considered the "spell" broken. My rose-colored glasses assured me that "happily ever after" would indeed be the ending to my tale.

46

More Kids

In our eighteenth year of marriage, we moved to a larger place, with the financial help of a very kind and generous relative. It was a beautiful 1912 Craftsman bungalow with an office detached from the house, where Troy's work didn't interfere with the normal noisy chaos of childhood. The kids seemed surprisingly well adjusted, despite all they had been through. None of them had yet reached adolescence, so we were experiencing the "sweet spot" of parenting, and none of the children showed any visible signs of trauma, which only confirmed, in my mind, that God was causing all things to work out for good. What didn't kill them was indeed making them stronger, and I was joyfully convinced that all our pain and struggles were paying off as God was proving himself faithful to complete the work He had started in us.

Troy was determined to regain favor with the pastors and redoubled his efforts to be a better husband and father in order to be considered a candidate, once again, for ministry. After eighteen years of being told no, he persisted. This could be considered a strength or yet another example of his narcissistic tendency to insist that he was right and everyone else was wrong. At this juncture, we believed "God was calling us" to add to our family, through adoption. It's humorous to me now that we couldn't simply have desires "just because." All expressed wants, in and of themselves, were idolatrous unless the Holy Spirit whispered the idea in our ear. Then it was acceptable. "We felt the Lord directing us . . ." "We sensed the Holy

Spirit telling us . . ." "We got a word from the Lord . . ." Since adoption was "God's idea," then our entire history of multiple counseling sessions for domestic abuse were magically swept under the rug, and the pastors and small group leaders offered their letters of recommendation and support.

In 2005, two precious little boys, ages three and four, biological brothers, joined our family, increasing our "quiver" to six.

Time to pause and let this sink in for a minute. After all we had been through—after so much pain and dysfunction—we believed our marriage and parenting skills were healthy enough to bring two traumatized children into it. The basis of our qualifications was our faith in Jesus. Our track record was irrelevant. The interviewing process was rigorous because social services wanted to make sure the kids were entering a safe and loving home. Fundamentalist Christians and the state often have different definitions of what "safe and loving" looks like. I never mentioned any past abuse of the kids or of myself because I truly believed it was ancient history and I fully trusted that God was using our parenting, as flawed as it was, for the good of the children. Besides, Troy had grown and changed and was not the same person he had been for the past eighteen years. I believed he was becoming less abrasive and more humble. He had seen the error of his ways, and I didn't feel it was necessary to dredge up the sins of his past. I was confident this next time around would be better, and we would get to see the difference that two decades of spiritual growth would make. When the social worker interviewed our biological children, we did exactly what families who have something to hide did: we coached them on what to say. We believed the greater good was to have an opportunity to raise these boys to know Jesus and ultimately receive eternal life. If that meant withholding information to the home-study professionals who wouldn't understand our Christian values and motives, so be it. We weren't going to throw our pearls of wisdom to the secular humanist swine. During the fostering process, we followed the rules to a tee and refrained from any hint of corporal punishment. But no sooner had we signed the adoption papers than our sweet, shy, frightened little boys were subjected to the same terrorizing intimidation that the older kids had endured. Within days of the adoption, some family friends had come over to visit. When our little guy bent over while playing, he showed his "plumber crack," and our friend's daughter, age five, announced that our son had "exposed his butt to her." Troy grabbed our son and whisked him off to the bathroom where his screams were heard throughout the house as he was severely spanked for something so innocent. Amidst heaving sobs and terror on his face, he had to apologize to the little girl and her parents, promising never to "show his bottom" again. They were so afraid of Troy that one time, the older one even pretended to be sick and forfeited a birthday party that he had been invited to when he discovered Troy would be the one driving him in the car instead of me. Grief-stricken, I thought, *My God, what have we done?* I wanted to save the lives of two little children, just as my parents had done. And yet unwittingly, by not disclosing our past issues, I had allowed these little boys to walk right into a land mine. I tried to understand how Troy could just repeat the same mistakes over and over again if the Holy Spirit was supposed to be refining him. Where exactly was this supernatural agent of change, making him more and more Christ-like? After all the counseling and interventions through the years and burying his dream of vocational ministry, after going through all the training classes on how to deal with children who have experienced trauma, could he not grasp what his behavior looked like and felt like to everyone else? And to see the terror on the faces of our new little boys was beyond unacceptable. By this time, I no longer felt obligated to helplessly watch with hands tied. I had to speak up and advocate for them. Our older kids had heroically found their voice as well, and we all stood together in solidarity, demanding change. Troy didn't like it one bit and would go for weeks at a time, refusing to back me up on any given decision, since "I didn't approve of his discipline methods." Eventually, though, with enough peer pressure, he stopped poking and jabbing and cracking his whip, to which everyone was relieved, and he officially retired the "rod of correction" several years ago, when he tried to spank our sixteen-year-old and she threatened to call the police if he ever struck her again. And as one might guess, the "Raise up the child in the way that he should go" promise we clung to with such vigor and hope proved to be inadequate as the older children's pain caught up with them, leading them each down their own angry, rebellious detours to escape and mask their devastating wounds. Through it all, I still believed that my relationship with Jesus was the greatest gift I could ever have and never stopped expressing joy in every circumstance, knowing that my savior was in control. I couldn't even imagine for a second how atheists could navigate through life's bumps without God. My story of early childhood neglect, crazy apocalyptic brainwashing, a dysfunctional marriage, domestic violence, and abusive parenting looked strangely perfect and even quite normal. To me it screamed of amazing grace and God's goodness. Joy unspeakable.

Part V

Born Again—Again

47

The Unraveling

So how does one go from loving Jesus for fifty years, teaching Sunday school, playing piano on the worship team, writing and directing the children's Christmas pageants, leading small groups, and training six kids in the faith to becoming a Unitarian Universalist, gay-loving, left-wing, secular humanist? Sorry! I should've announced, "Spoiler alert!"

It all started when my spirited and fiercely independent twenty-year-old daughter had just come home from a year-long excursion traveling through Europe. As she and I were standing in the kitchen, catching up, Kenzi, with a hint of contempt in her voice, kept referring to Christians in third person, "they" and "them." My heart reluctantly began deciphering the clues, but I didn't want to believe it. She was no longer a Christian. To an ultra-conservative, right-wing, "Focus on the Family" supporter who had devoted her life to raising up her children "in the Lord," such a revelation was unthinkable. How could my daughter, my flesh and blood, my little girl who was baptized at age twelve, who zealously defended God's honor amidst the skeptics in her public high school, not believe? Yeah, she had some close calls in the past, but she always managed to come around. When she was seventeen, she studied in Mexico as an exchange student. This was her first taste of freedom, and she took advantage of it, like a prisoner getting a temporary leave of absence from incarceration. She posted pictures of herself on Facebook toggling a cigarette in one hand, a red plastic party cup of alcohol in the other, while sandwiched between several young lusty Latinos with tongues seductively sticking out. My heart reverberated pure, raw, unadulterated fear. Where was my innocent little Christian girl with three hundred Bible verses committed to memory from her years in AWANA, whose eyes had been shielded from even PG-13 movies, and whose skills were being groomed to teach Sunday school and play the piano with the youth worship band? She was clearly on the wrong path, and I had to do something about it. So like any good fundamentalist parent, I rushed her a copy of *Seven Minutes in Hell* in her "(s)care package" just to warn her of what was in store for those who stray. Just as I had been terrorized my entire childhood, with the looming reality of hellfire, my knee-jerk reaction was to instill the same fear-based compliance in my own child. When she returned to the States, she went back to church, rededicated her life to Christ, and all was well again. Whew! But here we were, a few years later, and this time, she wasn't just experimenting or rebelling. She wasn't "sowing her wild oats." She had given the matter a lot of thought and had announced that she couldn't embrace Christianity because it purported that her beautiful atheist friends she had met in Europe were going to hell. She explained, "I've always heard that atheists were evil, immoral people who were incapable of goodness because they didn't have the Holy Spirit changing their wicked hearts. But then I met some, and they broke all the stereotypes. I've never met more kind and loving people in all my life. I just can't accept that they would be condemned to fiery torment forever and ever simply because they don't believe in an invisible deity, while some mean-spirited Christians would make the cut, simply because they do."

My daughter was making some good points, but my mind was in panic mode. As I was trying to process what she was saying, she delivered the death blow: "I don't care what the Bible says. [Whoa! Move over to escape the lightning bolt!] The idea of hell can't possibly be true, and if I have to believe it to be a Christian, I don't want any part of it."

Immediately, I reassured myself that this was only a phase. "Faith comes by hearing, and hearing by the Word of God." Once she was back in the pew, hearing the gospel, she would be flooded with truth and light again and all her questions and doubts would be absolved through her tears of repentance. My Christian family would be intact again, with no little lambs outside of the fold. My well-worn glasses assured me that all would be well because Jesus said so.

48

H.E. Double Hockey Sticks

Is He *able, but not willing?* Then He is malevolent.
Is He both able and willing? Then whence com-
eth evil?
Is He neither able nor willing? *Then why call Him
God . . .*

—Epicurus

From that brief conversation, I was on a mission to uncover answers and to help Kenzi find her way back to Jesus. I had recently read a book by Rob Bell called *Love Wins,* which suggested the possibility that everyone would ultimately make it to heaven. While I didn't believe it myself, I thought this might be a good start if she still wanted to be a Christian but was merely hung up on what happens in the afterlife. In a way, I didn't care too much about what she believed about hell. The most important thing in my mind was that she still believed in Jesus because the Bible was clear that He was the *only* way to God. If she could still hold on to her savior, hell would be a moot point. In other words, as long as *my* family and *I* made it, God could do whatever "the hell" he wanted with everyone else.

I started researching the doctrine of hell and the different positions Christians have historically held on the topic from annihilation to eternal conscious torment to ultimate restoration. Some believe that hell is punitive. Others see it as restorative. Another group believes it is just a metaphor to describe the alienation of being separated from God, while still others view hell as here on earth, when we experience evil or immense suffering. After watching YouTube videos, perusing recommended books, and listening to podcasts, my brain wrapped all the information I had just digested into a neat little package with a gift tag that said, in bold print, "**Oh my God! We don't really know**!" The holy, infallible scriptures that I leaned on offered multiple theories, with each one being embraced and defended by various brands of Christianity. How could I be certain which view was correct when there wasn't a consensus on the issue? Further, I learned that the word *hell* had been inserted into the scriptures much later and wasn't even in the original texts. My mind was about to explode. This immovable, belief, permanently cemented from childhood into my theological framework was starting to crack. Was it possible that my view of hell was wrong? Just the tiniest inkling of hope that I could be mistaken sent me on a six-month tangent of study, trying to gather enough information to justify letting this barbaric notion crumble and wash away into the vast sea of ancient superstition. Over the years, I had tried my best to wrap my brain around it, tried to put myself in God's shoes, tried to embrace my pastor's teaching that hell was necessary and was merely another reflection of God's perfect holiness. I tried to focus on my own unworthiness of being chosen, thanking God relentlessly for saving *me* even though my rescue was clearly undeserved. With tears in my eyes and hands lifted toward the heavens, I would gratefully sing, "Thank you for the cross! Thank you, Lord, for saving *me*, out of millions lost. Thank you, Lord, for saving *me*!" I tried to snuff out the "millions lost" part, because my heart and mind couldn't process that reality. I resigned myself to the fact that I may never understand or be okay with hell, but I would just have to trust in the goodness and wisdom of God. I had done everything I knew to do to raise all six kids to love and follow Jesus, and I would fight to the death for their soul if they ever became ensnared along the way. But suddenly, hell was a real threat again, and I could *never* be okay with anyone that I loved going there. Kenzi's de-conversion shook me to the core and exposed my own narcissistic attitudes toward God's gift of salvation. As long as I was saved, along with my family, I could detach myself from the unthinkable ramifications.

My mind was ripe and yearning for proof of a more triumphant, cosmic outcome of Christ's sacrificial death for mankind, one that would include hope for a wayward and confused twenty-year-old. Surely He didn't plan to only save a few, when the death of a deity warranted salvation for all. I found what I was looking for when I stumbled upon Christian Universalism, the very idea to which I had been introduced in elementary school by my Sunday school teacher but which had been promptly rejected as heresy due to my mom's emphatic reaction. When I first read Rob Bell's book, that spark of optimism was momentarily rekindled but immediately snuffed out by the angry reaction of mainstream Christianity. "How dare Rob Bell erase hell! He's playing with fire!" But then, when Kenzi showed up, renouncing her faith, the stakes became too high to refuse a closer look for myself. Before I knew it, I had read every book I could find on Christian Universalism, and it made sense. One night, as I was sitting at the computer reading excerpts from a website called "Hope Beyond Hell," I started to weep with joy and relief. Before this point, I thought I had only two options with regard to salvation: As an adult, my church's theology shifted from Arminian teaching to Calvinism. In my former tradition, I was taught that I must choose God (exercise my free will) in order to be saved, and I could lose my salvation at any moment by sinning. Hence, as a child, I lived in a perpetual state of fear, wondering if I had fallen out of favor with God. The remedy was to get "saved" over and over again by responding to the altar call at church. In this view, God "wants" to save everyone but is limited by man's free will. In other words, God doesn't get what God wants. But with reformed teaching (Calvinism), I was taught that God chooses us. We don't choose Him. In simplistic terms, this doctrine teaches that every single person in the human race from the time of Adam is born damned because of original sin. So the default position is that we are all hell-bound unless God, by His mercy, decides to rescue us. His choosing has nothing to do with how good or bad we are but simply by His own good pleasure. Further, if he chooses us, we are saved forever and nothing can separate us from the love of God. This, of course, is great news for a believer. My sincere and unrelenting trust in Jesus was the evidence that proved God had indeed chosen me, and so my eternal security was firmly established. Yet I couldn't seem to appease the nagging question that plagued my conscience: "If God could choose *me* to be saved, based on the work of Christ, apart from any personal merit, why couldn't he simply choose everyone to be saved by Christ's sacrifice?" The thought that God would allow His creation to suffer for eternity when he could do something about it and even claimed it was His desire was a troubling thought I couldn't rationally dismiss. How could an all-powerful, all-loving, and good God refuse to save his poor, helpless creatures when the death of His son supposedly had purchased salvation for all? Further, at what point is it possible for an unchanging, merciful God to cease being merciful?

Universalism was my golden ticket. This third model embraced elements of both traditions. It also held to the inerrancy of scripture and posited that God was one hundred percent triumphant over sin and death and that the curse would be lifted for all of mankind. This answered the plaguing questions and fears I had about the millions of people in Taiwan and the other billions around the planet who were doomed for not believing in Jesus or not even knowing about him. And the mentally disabled adults I cared for would make it. My sixth-grade bully, Judy, and the rebellious boy mentioned at camp would make it. Babies and Alzheimer's patients, my atheist Aunt Agnes, people with schizophrenia would be saved. No one I have ever known and loved would be turned away. The poor, starving children in Ethiopia, living a hopeless and bleak existence, would be welcomed into paradise. Everyone, everywhere, from every religion, culture, walk of life, age, occupation, or citizenship would be united forever, with hearts transformed and evil erased—a perfect utopia. I was undone. This was the best and most glorious version of the gospel I had ever heard. This God was worthy of being worshipped! His son's sacrifice was truly good news for the whole world. A veil had been lifted, and I could see the unity of the planet for the first time. I remember the next day driving to work and gawking at all the people in the cars in front, beside, and behind me. All I could think of was, "They are all going to be saved! Therefore, I have permission to love everyone and reject no one." I no longer divided people based on their religion, denomination, or lifestyle. We were *all* a part of the human race, and Jesus was going to save us all.

49

Testing the Waters

I knew these ideas weren't mainstream Christian orthodoxy, but my research assured me they most certainly existed in the teachings of early church fathers such as Origen of Alexandria and others but were later deemed heretical as other doctrines built momentum and attempted to weed out dissenting views. I reasoned, if even today, with literally thousands of commentaries, books, blogs, and sermons being written by brilliant apologists, seminarians, and pastors the world over trying to make sense of the same tired passages of scripture and yet not arriving at the same conclusions, there was room for differing ideas under the umbrella of Christianity. For the next days, weeks, and months, my love for those around me seemed to grow because the dividing walls had been removed and I was free to love the quirky eccentric, the drug addict, the hipster, the lesbian podcaster, the coffee partyer, and even the (gulp) atheist, without wondering if God would count my acceptance of certain individuals as treason against Him. I can say, this was one of the happiest seasons of my Christian faith. God became bigger and more victorious to me, and I naively thought other Christians, upon hearing this amazing news, would be as elated as I was. But it wasn't the case. The responses were inflammatory and reactive. "What about Hitler? Do you really want to bunk next to him for eternity?" "Some people deserve to rot in hell. I don't want them ruining heaven for me!" I couldn't let it go, though, even with the naysayers trumpeting their opposition.

50

A Trip to the Principal's Office

I wasn't convinced that my generous view of Christ's inclusiveness was evil. In fact, I thought Jesus might even be pleased with my gushing accolades over his celebratory butt-kicking of Satan. I desperately wanted to talk about it with my Christian friends, but the hints I had thrown out previously seemed to indicate that my message would not be well received. It took months for me to conjure up the courage to tell Troy, and his reaction was not surprising. He condescendingly dismissed my thoughts as childish and ridiculous. But deep down, he was afraid. He immediately went to the pastor and tattled that I was dabbling in heresy. I mean, how dare I believe for one moment that God would save *everyone*! Shame on me for giving God a five-star Amazon rating for overall deific performance. Pastor Mike reacted with the same grave concern.

"Oh, that's really bad! Get her into my office right away!"

Suddenly I was eleven years old again and being sent to the principal's office for "throwing snowballs during recess." My throat was dry. My hands were clammy. I had forgotten until now what it had felt like to get in trouble. I had always been a good girl because I hated confrontation, and here I was, a fifty-year-old mother of six with only a handful of speeding tickets to my otherwise clean rap sheet, reliving my childhood misdemeanors. What was I thinking to question the teachings of *the* church? By *the* church, I'm referring to the nondenominational community church, membership three hundred. You know, the "right" church—the true church. I was about to be stripped of my prestigious title, "pillar," and branded with the scarlet *H* for heretic, rendering me a dangerous threat to the body of Christ. I knew the meeting was a setup when Pastor Mike started the conversation with, "So, Joy, do you think you know more than your husband?" The correct answer would have been, "No, suh, Pasta Mike! I's jest a poor dumb woman in need of a man to teach me spitchel thangs." But instead, I meekly offered, "Well, I've read a lot of books on Christian Universalism, and I think I might have more information on the subject than he does." Pastor Mike responded patronizingly, "Oh, so you think you are an expert, do you?" Wow. He was good. Only two questions in, and he had me cornered. When I admitted that I wasn't an expert, he triumphantly went in for the kill. "So then, are you open to hearing what others have to say?" That seemed to be code for "Okay. Good. Shut up and let me tell you what you are supposed to think." When I nodded my consent, Pastor Mike then built his case by first insisting that the only supporting evidence we would look at would come from the Bible He would simply ask me to read the proof texts aloud and summarize. The problem with this method was that my reasons went far outside the bounds of the biblical text. The issue was interpretation, context, later interpolations, and conflict with other passages. There were also philosophical, historical, theological, emotional, and psychological considerations driving me to this conclusion. When attempting to explain my position, the pastor would laugh in a mocking way, as if to say, "Oh, you poor, poor, dear, deceived daughter of Eve!" He assigned me a book to read to set me straight and asked me to come back after I had read it for another discussion. This was not a discussion, though. It was clearly an intervention, and I knew when I left his office, I would read the book but would never subject myself to the humiliation of such a scenario again. I was comforted by the realization that out of seven billion people on the planet, only a tiny fraction of the population believed the way my pastor did. This helped me to see that he didn't have the corner on truth and I was under no obligation to adopt his views if it wasn't my conviction. I was starting to think for myself. I was giving myself permission to have my own ideas. While my gut warned me that this was a dangerous thing, my heart was joyfully pulsating the rhythm of freedom, and it was exhilarating.

51

The B-I-B-L-E Revisited

Journal, April 2014

I just can't help but think, if the Bible is true, inerrant, and without contradictions, the entire landscape of Christendom for two thousand years would look starkly different. The fact that so many holy men and scholars who devoured the scriptures, trying to interpret it correctly could not arrive at the same conclusions on matters of faith, piety, communion, baptism, salvation, the incarnation, the deity of Christ, the Trinity, the Sabbath, heaven and hell, original sin, women's roles . . . and the list goes on and on, leads me to believe that the book cannot possibly be divinely written. Even today, with thousands of seminary students around the world, continuing where the ancients left off, exegeting scripture, we are no closer to discovering any unified, or standardized message of every chapter and verse that all would agree upon. So this isn't even about the heathens and the Christians disagreeing. It's about Christians and Christians not seeing eye to eye and YET continuing to insist their good book is perfect, true, and God-breathed and we should all follow it.

In my search to find scholarly support for Christian universalism, I came across a plethora of articles, books, and videos calling into question the reliability of scripture and how many passages have simply been misquoted, mistranslated, forged, added to centuries later, and certainly misunderstood down through the ages. Bart Ehrman, a renowned biblical scholar and former Christian, turned atheist, has written several books that opened my eyes to the truth behind the Bible's less-than-immaculate origins. Equally shocking was the discovery that some of my favorite Bible stories weren't original but had been borrowed from other pagan myths. I also read how we got our canon of scripture, which is far from being "God-breathed." It was a council of men arguing over which books should make it in and which ones should be excluded. There were many gospels and acts that didn't make the cut, and some Bibles even have different collections of books. How does this fit in with the idea that the Bible is the infallible holy Word of God? Which version are we talking about? This begs another question: how could God's words be filled with inaccuracies and blatant contradictions? Robert Ingersoll's book, *Some Mistakes of Moses*, highlights countless errors in the Old Testament, which clearly make the collection of stories suspect, when claiming its authorship as penned by the Creator himself. Why would God allow his words to be changed and exposed to error? Why would his words be so confusing that literally thousands of commentaries have been written to try and make sense of it and still even the greatest and brightest theologians couldn't agree? Why would centuries and centuries of believers struggle with the meaning of texts to determine the correct interpretation? I read a shocking and horrifying story about one of the church heroes of the Protestant Reformation, John Calvin, who had his fellow Christian friend burned at the stake—*murdered*—for arriving at a different interpretation of a particular passage of scripture. They both loved God and both believed the Bible to be infallible. Surely the Holy Spirit should've provided the same enlightenment to both men for the verses in question. After all, both were earnestly seeking the truth, and yet one ended up on the rotisserie, giving the words "*Well done*, good and faithful servant" a whole new meaning. The questions I hadn't thought to ask, or had been afraid to ask, for almost fifty years started flowing. I couldn't dismiss them or try and stuff them away in a secret compartment of my brain to be silenced or smothered.

I knew I was on a slippery slope to question the inspiration of scripture, but my nagging questions got the best of me, and I continued searching out what leading scholars and historians had to say. I hadn't anticipated this shift of questioning. I merely stumbled upon it while attempting to find a theological system that could better explain the paradox of free will and God's sovereignty and give me a hope of God's ultimate plan of reconciliation for all mankind. The more I learned, the more I could see my childhood indoctrination song starting to morph. The tune was the same, but different lyrics were coming to mind. "The B-I-B-L-E, a bunch of ba-lo-ney, I don't believe it's the Word of God, the B-I-B-L-E." The cornerstone and foundation of my entire belief system was starting to shake. The evidence presented was whittling away at this massive, seemingly indestructible pillar. Before I knew it, it was teetering back and forth and ready to crash with a deafening thud. I tried to reinforce it with some theological scaffolding by pulling out the big guns to defend the Bible using logic and sound reasoning. I fully expected that the Christian apologists would dismantle the damning evidence for me and stabilize my foundational pillar once again. But even after watching hours and hours of debates by the best Christian defenders the Internet had to offer, such as Dinesh D'Souza, Douglas Wilson, and William Lane Craig, it seemed that the mountain of evidence was too convincing for me to hold on to my original belief. In my mind, the skeptics had won and biblical inerrancy seemed to shatter under the weight of science, historical facts, and reason. Without warning, my entire belief system crumbled before my eyes, leaving only smoke and ashes in its wake.

The video footage of the Twin Towers collapsing during the 9/11 attack is forever emblazoned on my brain. And it's this image that comes to mind when I think of the hit my belief system took when my confidence in the Bible disintegrated. Every other major doctrine was attached to and supported by truth claims from my Holy Book. When it collapsed, my entire worldview came crashing down with it.

Journal, 2-12-13

Right now, I can't seem to discern if what is happening to me is to be welcomed or shunned. At moments, I feel sheer joy and relief and a new sense of freedom. At other times, I'm paralyzed with fear and dread. All I can say is, everything I have believed in earnest for most of my fifty-one years of existence has been ripped away and dismantled from the iron-clad foundations that once held my assumptions firmly in place.

52

Looking Through the Rubble

I wondered what, if anything, could be salvaged from the rubble. Did I have any pillars still erect or even partially standing? What about the creation story? Are we, in fact, a product of intelligent design? If so, does he/she lay claim to our lives? For the first time, after dismissing evolution at the ripe age of eleven, I decided to take another look. I needed to find out why 99.8 percent of scientists validated this theory despite no sign of a croco-duck in the fossil record, as pointed out by the former child star turned Christian spokesperson, Kirk Cameron. Oh, I thought I had studied Darwin's crazy ideas as a Christian and felt confident in my original assessment that he was a God-hating, deluded liar who didn't even believe his own theory. The truth is, however, I only read about and listened to Christians such as Ken Ham, Kent Hovind, and Ray Comfort telling me why Darwin was wrong, feeding into my well-established confirmation bias. But now that my worldview was already demolished, it seemed appropriate to give the other side a legitimate chance to make its case. I read a book by Jerry Coyne entitled *Why Evolution is True*. Every page was backed with stunning evidence from the fossil record and more evidence from DNA. Claims made by the Christian right were addressed and effortlessly debunked. By the end of the book, I was absolutely convinced that I had been swinging from the wrong tree my entire life. Turns out, I'm a kin to the monkey after all (yeah, yeah, yeah)!

Next I tackled *A Universe from Nothing* by acclaimed physicist, Lawrence Krauss, explaining how, indeed, something could come from nothing, contrary to the Christian claim that God necessarily had to be the agent starting everything in motion. I devoured books and articles by Dan Barker, Karen Armstrong, Carl Sagan, and Neil DeGrasse Tyson. Never in my wildest imagination would I have ever predicted that I would be secretly reading literature authored by (whisper) atheists! But once I started, I was on a roll, devouring works from the four horsemen, Dawkins, Hitchens, Harris, and Dennett. I felt like a porn addict, concealing my stash of contraband and desperately hoping that I wouldn't get caught. I picked up the Bible's creation story again from the debris. There was *no way* this was the factual account, based on the solid scientific evidence. This magical story of the first people in a garden with an enchanted tree and a talking snake belonged with all the other creation myths from around the world. It was no longer a valid explanation for how we got here. And if there was no Adam and Eve, there was no original sin. And if there was no original sin, there was no need for Jesus! By this time, I wasn't just inching my way down the slippery slope. I was on a bobsled, careening down the Matterhorn full speed, and there was no Jesus to take the wheel.

53

Oh, God! Don't Get Me Started on Jesus!

When the Bible lost its power to sustain my faith to believe the impossible, the story of Jesus's miraculous birth and resurrection could no longer be supported either. Part of the unraveling of the Jesus narrative started when I learned that the same motif, the idea of deity coming to earth, part human, part divine, dying sacrificially and rising from the dead, is used many times in other ancient mythologies that predate Christianity, so the story isn't unique. I thought, *If I reject these myths because they are fictitious, how can I turn around and accept the Christian account as true?*

Further, none of the authors who penned the New Testament had ever met Jesus, nor had they met anyone who had known Jesus. Not even Paul was writing as a firsthand eyewitness, and so virtually everything written about the savior of the world is hearsay. I had always thought that the four canonical gospels were independent stories corroborating the events, but it as it turns out, Matthew and Luke copied from Mark but then embellished and added stories and verses to suit their own motives, theologies, traditions, and respective cultures. "John," who clearly wasn't one of the apostles, as people readily assume, penned his epistle at least a century later. After reading a dozen books or more on the historicity of Jesus and the origins of the New Testament, I was left with contradictions, forgeries, interpolations, competing theologies, misquoted prophecies, and story elements eerily similar to Osiris, Romulus, Apollonius, and Homer, to name a few. Virtually every piece of evidence in my case for Christ was debunked and dismantled so thoroughly that my Jesus pillar, fashioned as an old, rugged cross, had nothing left to prop it up and fell with such force and magnitude my whole world began to quake.

Before I knew it, everything that had been imparted to me in childhood as "gospel truth" was shattered and scattered to the four winds. I no longer believed in any of it. I didn't believe in Yahweh, his son Jesus, the infallible Bible, heaven, hell, demons, angels, salvation, six-day creation, the Rapture, or Armageddon. For the first time, my mind was completely untethered from the religion of my youth, and the questions that once had answers were back on the table for a second look. Fundamentalism had lost its grip on my brain, and I had never felt freer.

54

Meanwhile, Back at the Ranch

As one can imagine, this "natural disaster" completely obliterating my core could not stay contained within my heart and mind. It began to spill out in my family. It started when Troy had scheduled our next interrogation with Pastor Mike regarding my heretical views about universalism. With every ounce of courage I could muster, I told him that I would not be meeting with Mike about the issue. A wave of guilt washed over me. I was saying no to my husband. I immediately started trembling as I saw Troy's countenance change. The old Troy—the angry, controlling Troy—was back with a vengeance. I hadn't seen this side of him for a while because I had finally figured out that, after so many painful years of trial and error, if I simply agreed with him and didn't make a fuss, we could have a decent relationship. But this was something I just couldn't agree to, and so I had no choice but to defy his orders. Next thing I knew, I was in a hostage situation once again as he forced me on the couch refusing to let me go until I had satisfied his demands for answers. By this time, universalism was a moot point because while I could still accept the possibility of an historic human Jesus, a man/god who came back to life and disappeared in the clouds was out of the question. How could I possibly admit to Troy that my apostasy was far worse than he could ever imagine? I didn't have words yet to describe what was happening internally because everything was moving so fast and the collapse of my faith was rather sudden, literally catching me off guard. The only words I could offer Troy were that I was going through my own season of searching and wasn't ready to disclose my thoughts with him or with Pastor Mike. Every red flag that could be raised went up, and Troy's veins were starting to pop again in his neck and forehead. He and the pastors had been ordained by God to provide my spiritual covering, since I was so easily deceived, what with being a woman and all. And there I was, off doing my own thinking, opening myself up to Satan's attack without even "checking in," goddammit! Troy, in a state of panic, accused me of having an affair. I asked incredulously, "How in the world could you make such a leap—from me questioning my theology to jumping in bed with someone else?" He retorted, "Because I can't trust you! You have secrets! You are going around behind my back and you refuse to tell me what's going on! Why wouldn't I think you are fucking someone else?" I assured him that I wasn't and told him I would talk to him after I had had a chance to formulate my thoughts. In my nervousness, I saw Troy's finger pointing in my face and his ranting, almost comical. I tried to hold back an involuntary grin, but Troy saw it and got even more angry. He stormed out of the house and slammed the door as I collapsed on the couch, shaking uncontrollably.

This was the first time I had ever refused to meet with the pastor or comply with Troy's spiritual directives, and so it isn't surprising that he would overreact out of fear. I tried to come clean by writing him a thirty-page letter/essay, attempting to articulate my struggles and doubts, which he promptly dismissed on the grounds that I was just too gullible. He claimed there were answers to every question I had raised, if only I cared to listen. But I had already heard the "answers" and had listened to the rebuttals. I just wasn't satisfied. After that, I had no desire to continue talking with him about it, and he was afraid to bring up the subject, so it became yet another elephant in the room that we simply avoided for the sake of peace.

55

Coming Out

When I shared with my daughter Kenzi that my search to win her over to Jesus had backfired, she was truly elated. For the first time, I felt like dividing wall we had between us had crumbled, along with my faith, and we could now love each other without any manipulative strings attached. I no longer felt compelled to keep pointing out her sins and coercing her through fear and guilt. I could accept her just as she was and love her without judgment or duty to correct. The effect was immediate as she began to open a dialogue with me, far deeper than we ever could've had with the constraints of religion stifling our connection. Since then, we have never been closer, and I am in awe of this beautiful, smart, articulate offspring of mine who led me out of a lifetime of mental captivity. For the other kids, I didn't want to dissuade them from their faith but also couldn't bear having them live another minute, thinking that they had to worry about hellfire. When I shared with them that I no longer saw any sufficient evidence for hell, the collective sigh of relief could've filled a hot air balloon. By allowing them all permission to think, question, search, and not blindly accept stuff without evidence, they all shed their faith like a wool blanket on a summer day. The results were dramatic and invigorating as we all found a new freedom to relate on deeper and more honest levels, with fundamentalism scoured from our language.

When the entire family defected, Troy's fragile ego took quite a hit. Not only had he been disqualified from becoming a pastor, he believed he had failed miserably in even shepherding his own family. For a while, he sent weekly emails to the kids, sharing a passage of scripture or a spiritual insight and always ending with an application to love God with heart, mind, and soul. But one by one, as the kids expressed their lack of faith and even posited their active atheism, he stopped writing altogether. He sent one final message, saying that he was a terrible father and that he wasn't going to send any more weekly letters because he was sure nobody read them anyway. I know I should be empathetic, but damn. All I heard was a tiny violin and passive-aggressive, guilt-inducing manipulation.

56

Dismembered

Journal Entry

Every waking moment, my mind is hijacked by an insatiable and intense craving for truth—not mythical or faith-based assumptions but observable reality—hard facts. There is so much we don't know and likely can't know, such as what happens when we die, or how did consciousness evolve, but I'm no longer able or willing to employ the god of the gaps theory to explain what I don't yet understand. Instead, I'm inclined to focus on what we can and do know, based on evidence, and make that my starting point for rebuilding my worldview.

On the inside, this incredible transformation was quietly and secretly taking place, while on the outside, I was still perceived as a Christian wife, Christian mother, Christian teacher, Christian songwriter, Christian neighbor, Christian family member, and of course, Christian friend. It was becoming increasingly difficult to carry on these roles when my entire motherboard was being rewired, detecting and quarantining religious indoctrination as a dangerous spyware. I desperately wanted to tell others, besides my children, what was happening internally, but this, to me, seemed riskier than coming out as gay or being exposed for infidelity. I was rejecting Jesus Christ: the only Way, the only Truth, and the only Life.

I started "liking" book titles I had been reading from authors like Sam Harris, Bart Ehrman, Dan Barker, Seth Andrews, and Robert Ingersoll on social media, as a way of putting my feelers out. I explicitly refrained from posting anything from Hitchens and Dawkins, to keep a low profile. I figured if someone else had been reading from my booklist, they might be going through a similar crisis and might initiate a conversation. And if not, they probably wouldn't even take notice. I certainly wouldn't have recognized any of the authors or titles had I not been ravenously hungry for answers beyond the aisles of Lifeway Christian Bookstore. But one day, I got a call from Phil, the senior pastor. Without mixing words, he said, "Some church members are concerned about what you are posting on Facebook. We need to talk." My heart started racing. My hands began to tremble. My mouth went dry. I almost started to cry. I had been busted and, once again, felt like a young child being sent to the school office for a paddling. This was revealing of how much power I had given the pastoral leaders and the degree of censorship endorsed by the church. I was so nervous I could hardly eat or sleep. When a middle-aged woman is gripped with fear over talking to her pastor about what she has been learning and thinking, one must conclude that there is an unhealthy cult-like relationship at play. When we finally met, thankfully, he was kind and gracious as he asked me to explain what was going on. I confessed that I was having some intense doubts and shared a bit of my recent struggle. He assured me that I wasn't alone and that everyone from time to time wrestles with his or her faith. But when I couldn't say I knew for certain that the Bible was inerrant, Jesus was born of a virgin, died on the cross for my sins, and ascended into heaven, Pastor Phil felt it was best that I withdraw my membership from the church. What a relief! I would no longer be asked to teach Sunday school or do things that now created a conflict of conscience. At the same time, I couldn't help but feel the sting of rejection—being ousted from the only "club" that I had identified with since I was a small child. The ramifications of my diversion from my prescribed script were catching up, and the barricaded "me" was becoming exposed. In the next weekly bulletin, sent to the members via email, Pastor Phil wrote the following:

> It is with much sadness that we announce the withdrawal of Joy [_]'s membership. In recent conversation Joy has informed me that she has significant doubts about the authority of scripture and by implication the truth of the gospel. She is going through a serious season of searching and questioning. It is our sincere desire that this dear friend will continue to attend church and home group. The elders also want to thank Joy for her service to our church. She has blessed us with her gifts of music and hospitality. Please befriend Joy and pray that God will renew her faith in the veracity of scripture and the wonder of the gospel.

While kind sentiments, neither he nor his wife have ever spoken to me since.

57

Just Believe!

Journal Entry

Christianity is slipping through my fingers and I don't know if I am to hold on for dear life or to let it go. If I'm wrong, the stakes are infinitely high. It's not that I choose not to believe. And it's not that I don't WANT to believe. I simply CAN'T believe without evidence. A naturalistic explanation for the origins of life seems to most consistently line up with empirical scientific evidence, yet I continue to find myself terrified at the remote possibility that the Bible, though flawed, is still true and that I am risking eternal conscious torment by my unbelief. I realize my fear is irrational, as I replay the evidence over and over again but my forty-eight years of indoctrination have left some deep grooves in my psyche, making it difficult to veer onto a more reasonable path.

After withdrawing my membership from church, I continued to attend the north campus, led by the associate pastor, with Troy and the young boys, for another six months, partly to preserve my reputation within the community and also to maintain, at least superficially, the only way of life I had ever known. I had no other place to fit in and no other culture with which I could identify. Even though in my gut, I knew I didn't believe, I wasn't ready to go public, and so I continued to pretend that my struggle was just a little bump in the road. It became increasingly uncomfortable with each passing week, though, and I knew it was just a matter of time before I would have to tell Troy that I couldn't do it anymore. The song lyrics, the Bible reading, the sermons continued to highlight a message all too familiar and yet now strangely foreign. I couldn't stop the busy chatter in my brain, providing an ongoing commentary on what was happening. "Please stand for the reading of God's Word." *How can I stand? I don't believe the Bible is God's Word!*

"We are poor wretched sinners deserving of hell for all eternity."

Bullshit! You are scaring an entire room of mindless sheep into submission and obedience by threatening an unspeakable act of terror. Shame on you!

"But unimaginable bliss awaits those whom God has chosen!"

Really? We are supposed to worship a god who just randomly chooses people, willy nilly, for his team like a Saturday game of kickball in the park, only the losers get tortured forever?

"So how do we know we've made it on God's happy list? If we believe."

But wait. That's it? Just believe? I thought we had to be chosen! Which one is it? Huh? Why is no one questioning this load of crap? And how is it possible to JUST believe, anyway? Our beliefs don't simply happen in a vacuum. We believe because our experience or observation confirms it, someone we trust has told us, or the evidence is such that we are persuaded. Without evidence, there is no such thing as 'just believe'!

The last straw for me, was attending on Communion Sunday when the entire church made their way to the front to receive the sacraments. This was a "meal" available strictly to believers, and to partake without being "right with God" would heap damnation onto the unworthy participant. I could've gone forward to bolster my charade because I had no fear whatsoever in the bogeyman curse, but I didn't *want* to go forward. This cannibalistic ritual, which at one time produced tears and deep, heartfelt emotion, no longer seemed to tug on my heartstrings. A year earlier, I had even written a beautiful song that was sung during the ceremony to help enhance the holy experience. For the first time since being allowed to take communion at the age of eleven, I decided to refrain and remained seated while at least a dozen people in our theatre-style seating had to crawl over me to get to the "Lord's Supper." As each member struggled past, trying not to step on my feet or accidentally land in my lap, I imagined the creative conversations going on in their heads. *Why isn't she going up? Does she have unconfessed sin in her heart? Has she not reconciled with someone who has offended her? Is she . . . not a believer?* I expected to feel embarrassed and uncomfortable because of my compulsive desire to "fit in" but instead experienced a strange surge of exhilarating defiance.

Ooh! This is new! I thought. My bad-girl image felt kind of titillating! They could think whatever their mental models wanted to conjure up, but I knew my days at this local fellowship were numbered. I just couldn't continue as a wolf in sheep's clothing. I didn't belong there anymore, and I knew it.

58

I Love You, UU

I had just read Jerry DeWitt's wonderful book, *Hope beyond Faith*, and had listened to podcasts about his launching of atheists churches around the country called the Sunday Assembly. I was not only intrigued but also ecstatic. I loved the social structure of church, meeting together with like-minded folks, forming a community of compassion and care, doing service projects, and giving and receiving support during times of personal crisis. I thought if I could keep the meeting and sense of community but throw out the dogma, I might feel less displaced in the world. I looked online to see if any such group existed in my neck of the woods. The only secular congregation that popped up in my search was the Unitarian Universalist (UU) Church. It claimed that everyone regardless of religious affiliation or lack thereof was welcome. I couldn't even imagine what "worship services" would look like without one specific deity as the primary focus, but I was irresistibly curious to find out. I waited for a Sunday when Troy was out of town to slip away and investigate, since I hadn't yet announced my departure from our old church. The service was very different from anything I had ever experienced. Its calm, hypnotic vibe with the lighting of the chalice and the candles of care, a gong for meditation, and hippie folk music playing during the offertory left me cocooned in a chrysalis of soothing peace. I nearly gasped when a candle was lit for the LGBTQ community's annual Pride festivities. I couldn't believe they weren't speaking in opposition to gay rights but instead they were offering their full love and support. A smile spread across my eager face. This, in my mind, was what church was supposed to be. Their focus on civic responsibility, human rights, compassion, and social justice were the very things I could wrap my mind, heart, and energies around, without any internal conflict. The sermon, more like a lecture, was intellectually stimulating and void of any manipulative overtones intended to convince or sell me on a bill of goods. I left the meeting feeling lighthearted and "fed" somehow, even though there was no mention of Bible God in any of the readings and reflections. Still, I wrestled with thoughts like, *You are heading to the dark side, the point of no return.* And *Don't you know, this is a pagan religion? Be careful! You are being deceived! But,* I reasoned, *if loving my neighbor and embracing peace was wrong, then I would just have to be damned.* This gathering radiated warmth for my soul, and like a fly, mesmerized by the porch light, on a summer evening, I too was drawn in, willing to risk getting zapped for the joy of being soothed momentarily by the aura. I continued to secretly attend the early service under the guise of going to my Weight Watcher meeting and contemplated how I could ever come clean with Troy.

My life, being swept along in a current too powerful to resist, was taking me further and further from the dock to which my boat had once been anchored. I couldn't turn around. Couldn't head upstream. I had to keep going. And of all the things I never imagined I would say or do or think, there I was, surprising myself at every turn. Who was this person who refused to meet with the pastor because she was unwilling to be intimidated and invalidated? Who was the Joy who courageously admitted to her husband that she had doubts? How would she now find her voice and tell Troy that she could no longer attend Sunday services with him and the boys? It wasn't optional. I couldn't keep going because I didn't believe. I could either sneak around and live a lie or walk in the light and tell Troy that I needed a new place to belong. I had no choice but to follow the truth of my conscience.

One Sunday, during lunch at a little fast food Mexican chain, I took a deep breath and decided to just rip the Band-Aid off quickly.

"So, Troy, I have been checking out a new church that I would like to start attending regularly." Troy was visibly surprised and even hopeful. He said, "Oh really? What church is that?" My lungs felt weak, unable to sustain enough air to offer my reply, so with some added force, I blurted rather unnaturally, "It's the Unitarian church right beside the community college." I tried to sound cheery and casual to mask my fear. There was a pause as Troy's expression turned to a scowl. Inhale. Exhale. I braced myself for the attack.

"The Unitarian Universalist church? [mocking laugh] The church which doesn't talk about God? [another mocking laugh] The church whose hymnal has no songs about Jesus? [voice escalating] The church that believes that anything goes [throws hands in the air] and it doesn't matter what you believe [lips starting to purse]? You can't get any more heretical than that!"

I decided this wasn't a good time to also mention that the minister was an atheist!

"They simply welcome all faiths and believe that truth can be found in many religious traditions and sources, not just one." I responded carefully. Pure, unadulterated disgust was written on Troy's countenance. When he had nothing left to say, he just got up and stormed out of the restaurant. Our son, Dakota, who had also been attending Buddhist meditation classes on Monday evenings at the UU church, smiled, offered a high-five, and said, "Well, that went well!" It hadn't gone as horribly as I had imagined, and I sat for a minute, steadying my breathing and smiling, feeling tremendously relieved that I had done yet another spine-tingling hard thing on my path toward authenticity.

A few weeks later, inspired by the minister Todd's sermon on embracing doubt and being at peace with the "mystery," I went home and penned the following poem that I read at the women's retreat a few weeks later. The huge tsunami in my mind, washing away every pillar and anchor, was starting to recede, and my poor shell-shocked soul was finding a gentle reprieve. After a desperate and obsessive two-year search for truth and following the truth wherever it took me, I was finally ready to take a breath and rest. What an enormous relief to be okay without answers and to admit that there were things that couldn't be known. *Agnostic* was no longer a scary bad word. It simply meant I was done pretending to know what I couldn't know.

My Truth, the Only Truth

I once claimed I "knew" the way
To paradise and how to pray
"Our Father in Heaven, hallowed by thy name"

I "knew" the narrow road of pain
That guaranteed eternal gain
Like mansions and riches if I didn't complain

I "knew" just how the world began
A flash of light with a voice command
And what God did to fashion man

I claimed to "know" the truth from lies,
And sentenced millions to their demise
Eternal torment for being blind

My truth, the only truth
My way, the only way,
My faith, the only faith
And everyone else was wrong

I once claimed I "knew" God's thoughts
About what is and what is not
"Thus saith the Lord," I was dutifully taught.

I "knew" the beginning and the end
While philosophers could only pretend
To understand or comprehend

The deepest unveiled mysteries
Were solved by my theology
How lucky truth was revealed to me.

I "knew" the things that can't be known
Like gates of hell and heaven's throne—
Life beyond this earthly home

My truth, the only truth
My way, the only way,
My faith, the only faith
And everyone else was wrong

My holy book said I "must" believe
No room for doubt lest I be deceived
Enticed by the adversary's schemes

So I dug in my heels and covered my ears
Closing my mind suppressing my fears
And held onto my truth, as sacred and dear

My truth, the only truth
My way, the only way,
My faith, the only faith
And everyone else was wrong

But then the doubts came creeping in
Like noise behind walls, paper-thin
I tried to repent of such egregious sin

But the doubts kept coming, assaulting my truth
Invading like a military coup
Demanding evidence, asking for proof

Alas my "knowing" lay bare and ashamed
For it had no support to make its proud claims
And all that was left was its hollow remains

My truth, the only truth
My way, the only way,
My faith, the only faith
Could it be I was wrong?

The greatest minds of humanity
Have contemplated life's mysteries
Yet with no consensus of certainty

So how could I insist to "know"
What even scholars couldn't show?
I had to let my assumptions go

My mind is unleashed, now free to explore
Investigate, study, discover, implore,
Unshackled unchained, an open door

To say "I don't know" is to say I am free
To embrace the beauty of mystery
And follow the evidence wherever it leads

My truth not the only truth
My way not the only way
My faith not the only faith
All this time I was wrong

59

Taking off the glasses

I never imagined in my wildest rabbit trails of thought or fantasy that I would find myself here at this moment, attending a Unitarian Universalist Church and calling myself a happy agnostic/atheist. My daily dose of joy is not contingent upon distorting reality or holding onto the promise of a magical utopian afterlife. I am at peace because I'm living authentically, allowed to feel what I really feel, think what I really think. There are no more fences keeping me in the same chewed and regurgitated pastures. No dividing walls barring me from loving and befriending anyone and everyone I meet. No more toxic threats paralyzing me with fear and spreading like a flaming torch to torment those around me in the name of "love." No more self-loathing, repenting, and groveling to please an invisible deity. No more strained relationships stifled by confrontation and spiritual accountability. As I've replayed the major scenes of my journey from childhood to the present, I see that religion and my rose-colored glasses provided the omniscient authority overriding my own internal voice. When my instincts said, "Run," my faith told me to stay. When I wanted justice, my external compass said, "Forgive." When my soul was numb and unresponsive, my spirit guide said, "Fake it." The distortion of my glasses convinced me to love what I hated (Bible studies and accountability) and to hate what I loved, (validation and acceptance), to call evil (domestic violence) good and to call good (defending my children) evil. At every turn, my still small voice was drowned out by religious indoctrination telling me what to think, how to act, and what to feel. Further, the message of the gospel, intended to bring me great peace, left me terrorized and scarred throughout my childhood and young adulthood. Yet I believed that the only way to unspeakable joy was through Jesus. In a way, it was true because the more I saw my own depravity, the sweeter the message of the Gospel became, and I often wept with deep gratitude that my sins had been forgiven and that I was heaven bound. Now I weep for that vulnerable little girl whose beliefs kept her small, anxious, and mistrusting because of terrible ideology. From the pain and ashes, though, has come rebirth and new beginnings. The following journal entry encapsulates this imagery in a nutshell.

Journal, April 2015
Burial and Rebirth

When I was sixteen, the real me died. I was dunked under water and symbolically buried in a sacrament called baptism. Why? Because I was born sinful, broken, and evil, like every other *Homo Sapien* who had gone before me. The real me, so I was told, hated God and could never please Him because my heart was stony and cold. Every part of my natural flesh, from my first cry out of my mother's womb, was tainted with transgressions, inherited from humanity's first parents. I wasn't a sinner because I had sinned. I sinned because I was inherently a sinner.

While my dirty, rotten carcass was left in her watery grave, just as the bloody, broken Jesus was dead in the tomb after taking on the sins of the world, a new and improved avatar emerged, not born of flesh but of spirit. The new me loved God and wanted to please him and had the Holy Spirit living inside, directing my path, convicting me of sin and helping me to please my Heavenly Father.

While the Bible seemed to imply that the death to my carnal self was instantaneous and final, it wasn't the case at all. It's more like she was continually trying to come up for air, only to be shoved back down and subdued, over and over again. The process of being conformed, molded, and shaped into the image of Christ entailed a slow excruciating lifetime of being "put to death" through rebuking, ignoring, suppressing, and resisting every thought or attitude that didn't align with my new nature. "He (Jesus) must increase and I must decrease," was my spirit-imposed battle cry.

With my new identity, I built a life around the church, the Bible, Jesus, and the promise of eternal bliss. I married a Christian, birthed four amazing kids, and adopted two more of equal valor. My highest calling was to serve my family and the local church. I dutifully read the Bible, prayed, shared the gospel, sent my kids to AWANA, endured discipline and correction from spiritual leaders, gave 10 percent of my income to the church, went on mission trips, made Jesus and others my priority, and denied my own needs and desires lest I be deemed selfish. I believed what I was told to believe without questioning and thought what I was instructed to think, in order to avoid the fires of hell.

But when my faith and dogma, the foundations upon which my spirit life was built, came crashing down in a heap of ruins, I realized the person I had become could only be sustained and realized through the religion that had created her. The chains that held my thoughts captive and forced me into a narrow, rigid view of the world fell off, freeing my mind to enjoy a smorgasbord of unrestricted, uncensored inquiry.

The young girl buried with Jesus in the church baptismal has come to the surface, allowed to breathe and feel and exist for the first time without being viewed a parasite or malignant virus.

This past year has been a season of incredible self-discovery. I'm getting to know the real me, and in many ways, I like the person looking back in the mirror. The kindness, generosity, compassion, and loving acceptance I have always felt toward others remained, even after the Holy Ghost vanished, leaving me to believe that many of my positive traits had always been a part of my natural DNA and not necessarily the product of religious indoctrination.

I'm also aware that maybe the preachers were right, on one level. The natural "me" doesn't like the notion of a vindictive God very much, at least not the Christian one, as was predicted and forewarned at every altar call. But I don't think it's my sin nature at work. It's the fact that the evidence for a personal deity is lacking. I would still worship Him if I could find any undeniable proof at all that He is real, but He has yet to come forward and identify Himself. And if he is the guy in charge, he has some serious explaining to do. As my avatar slowly makes her exit, I also find myself no longer driven to endless Bible studies, prayer meetings, and evangelistic outreaches. There is no more weeping for the salvation of my children and lamenting that a Democrat is in office (Update: Now I'm weeping that a narcissistic Republican is running the show!) I refuse to read Bible commentaries or prepare Sunday school lessons that perpetuate the lie that the precious children I am teaching are worthy of eternal conscious torment. I no longer believe it's appropriate to hit children or refuse rights based on sexual orientation. I don't think the world is about to come to an end or that I'm going to be whisked up into the clouds in the Rapture. I have no desire to scare my children into submission with threats of being rejected on the Great and Terrible Day of Judgment. I have no fear of demons lurking in the shadows waiting to devour me. Contrary to my avatar's scientific bent (or lack thereof), I'm now quite certain the world is more than six thousand years old, climate change is a thing, and evolution is true. Without the glue and mortar of religious rhetoric, much of what I once thought and believed can no longer stick and has since fallen by the wayside.

While it's a scary venture to set my soul free in all her humanness and imperfections, I have never felt more alive and whole by letting go of my avatar and embracing the tangible flesh and blood "me" that is made up of stardust, as Carl Sagan, put it, rather than the pixie dust of make-believe. I died at age sixteen but came back to life at fifty! This time, I truly feel "born again."

So ... What about Troy?

G ood question. Do you want the long version or the short one? The first invokes another thirty pages of me gathering the courage and clarity to ask for a divorce and accepting the painful ramifications of leaving a narcissist. The short version is, I eventually succeeded and now I'm happily moving forward. But perhaps, for the sake of closure, we could meet somewhere in the middle.

Troy had softened over the years, yet his propensity for violence still lingered under the radar and it only took a little bump for it to resurface. It was only recently that we were sitting at Starbucks with our daughter Savannah and I gently disagreed with something he said about our exchange student living with us from Spain. The fact that I wouldn't side with him made him so angry he jumped up, stood behind me, and put me in a chokehold while spewing a vitriolic monologue of mockery.

"So that's how you love me? That's how you show it? Thank you soooo much! I just feel soooo loved! You're the best wife ever!"

"Get your hands off my mom!" Savannah screamed. "You can't treat people that way!" With red face, trembling hands, and the same familiar veins pulsating from his temples, he eventually let go, grabbed his full cup of coffee, and dumped it in the trash, while spilling its contents on the floor along the way, and stormed out, as the noisy, crowded, bustling cafe fell silent to watch the terrifying commotion. Savannah reacted with the intensity I probably should have felt, but I just sat there numb and detached, waiting for him to stop his ranting so we could slip out without making a bigger scene. It was telling of how desensitized I had become after nearly thirty years and also confirmed to me that despite his progress, my mind would never register him as safe.

Last year, Troy took all the community cash, very large disbursements given to us from his parents from oil investments, and started a truck repair business and other secondary businesses in North Dakota during the oil boom in the Bakken. He was gone for several months at a time, as the businesses got off the ground, coming home for only 3–7 day intervals. It was during his months away that the kids and I had a chance to experience the climate change when Troy was home, versus when he was in North D. The boys were much happier and more relaxed and even lamented the days their dad would be home again. During his time away, he never once called the kids or even asked about them, and so it seemed the feelings were mutual.

Divorce had never been on the table and was deemed a non-viable option even in the latter of "for better or worse" possibilities. I was no quitter, and I could withstand the harshest of relational conditions. I had weathered years of storms and turmoil and was all the stronger for it. There was no reason I couldn't just keep on keeping on with gritted teeth and sheer willpower. But the question I had not asked until now was, "Do I want to?" What I wanted and needed wasn't a part of my fundamentalist Christian toolbox. The only question I was allowed to ask was, "What does God want and need?" God wanted and needed me to stay married until death. He said so himself apparently, and who was I to argue with God? But now that the Bible no longer held me in its paralyzing grip, the yearning in my own gut to live wholeheartedly and authentically took centerstage, and I knew that staying in a marriage that couldn't allow the freedom to express my true self was a death sentence to the "me" I was just getting to know. Still, I tiptoed lightly and cautiously around the idea, simply posing the "What if" question. It wasn't that I was getting a divorce. But *what if* I did? As I allowed this once captive thought to be unleashed into the wild, I started to laugh because I had flashbacked to my de-conversion when I had asked the same question and ended up divorcing God. I knew if I could let go of my savior, whom I had loved and feared since childhood, the ultimate abuser who constantly threatened me with hell, then Troy didn't have a fighting chance!

After thirty years of being locked in a prison of unworthiness, hustling for the right to belong, and resigned to a life sentence of "less than," I saw the light. The warm beams of truth squeezed in between the bars, shining fiercely into my core and revealing, for the first time, what had been hidden for decades. I was worthy of being loved, just as I was. I didn't deserve to be marginalized, abused, and controlled. From that earthshattering revelation sprang a host of chain reactions, all set in motion to center me in truth and offset the imbalance my faulty thinking had created.

Because I had been processing our relationship in his absence and finding myself at a place of restlessness, it was no surprise that I felt more disconnected than usual from Troy when we were reunited for our daughter's wedding in New York City. I was guarded with him, and he in turn responded with hostility. Amidst the beauty and magic of cruising along the Hudson River in an old turn-of-the-century wooden yacht, complete with the bride and groom, happy guests, Statue of Liberty, and Manhattan skyline in the distance, I felt only coldness, rudeness, and brooding from Troy. It was obvious he was mad when he didn't even sit by me at dinner or dance with me during the reception. But in keeping with our thirty-year tradition, nothing was addressed. We simply ignored the giant elephant of our creation and carried on with business as usual. When he headed back to North Dakota after the wedding, I don't remember him even kissing me goodbye. He just got up and said, "I guess I'll see you in three months." And that was that. The sound of eggshells under my feet was like nails on a chalkboard. I couldn't take it anymore. If after three decades, we still couldn't share what we were thinking and feeling, still suppressing our emotions, we didn't have a real marriage. I was done pretending. I wanted out.

When he returned in September, he was only planning to be physically home for two days out of the entire week because he was going backpacking with some friends. On the one night he was home,

I asked if he wanted to go out to a restaurant and catch up. The conversation was stilted and flat. I tried to ask him about the businesses and life and relationships. He answered dryly as if being forced into a customer satisfaction questionnaire following an uneventful hotel visit. During the entire meal, he did not think to ask even one question about me, how I was doing, if I needed anything, or if there was something wrong, considering the tension was thicker than the cheesecake on our plates. He said he was planning on opening two more repair shops. I did the math. If the first one took a year to get running, the others would theoretically require the same amount of time. That meant he wouldn't be coming home for several years. In my mind, the marriage was over. It was time to make my move. But because he left no open door to even address what was going on internally with me, I figured I would have to wait until his next visit at Christmas or even later so as not to spoil the holiday. The night before his scheduled departure, we hosted a huge neighborhood barbecue in the backyard. I left a list on the counter of things I needed him to do while I was at work because once I got home, I would only have an hour and a half to set up a party for eighty-plus guests. But when I got home, the list was untouched. He hadn't seen it, and so I had to quickly shift into to overdrive, with no time for cushioned *please*'s and *thank-you*'s and "Would you mind?" with each request. It was ninety minutes of all hands on deck, working frantically and furiously.

The next morning, when he was supposed to leave, he complained that I had never treated him as rudely and horribly as I had the night before. The funny thing is, I only remember having two very brief interactions all evening. One, he asked where to put the water bottles, and I said, "On that table." The other time, I asked if he knew where the remote was for the video player because the outdoor movie was about to start. He just shrugged and said, "I don't know," and left me to try and figure out a solution. But those two conversations were apparently the worst I had ever treated him. Because I wasn't polite enough to his satisfaction, he immediately jumped to the worst-case scenario. He asked accusatorily, "Who are you fucking in my bed?" This was the second time he had questioned my fidelity, and both times were rooted in fear because I had behaved in a way that threatened his sense of control over me.

His offensive accusation brought the final death blow, snuffing out any remaining pulse, but also provided the open door I was looking for. Like doing the polar plunge off the ship in Antarctica, I had to turn off my brain and go into autopilot. *Don't think. Don't second-guess. Just jump!* And I did. I opened my mouth, and the words spilled out. I said, "Troy, I love you and I love me, but I don't love *us*. Our marriage no longer works for me. I want a divorce." I said it and I couldn't take it back.

If there was any doubt that I had made the right decision, I need only look at the subsequent days and weeks after the divorce announcement to see how his manipulative behavior was eerily similar to our first years of marriage. The moment he felt he had lost power over me, he pulled out all the stops to reestablish control. The master bedroom was suddenly his domain, and he forbade me to even touch the ceiling fan, reminiscent of the car radio decades before. When I moved my hand toward it to turn on the light, he screamed, "I said *do not* touch the fan!" And with that, he grabbed the beaded chain and completely yanked it off, as it slithered and went limp in his fist, to ensure that I would never disobey his orders. He then started violently removing the printer from my workstation and dismantling my desk, shoving it in the spare room that was already full of our daughter and son-in-law's belongings being stored temporarily while they were on their honeymoon. I needed my desk, computer, and printer as I was doing lesson plans for my teaching job and begged him to wait until I could move out of the room properly. He refused to stop as we continued to play tug-of-war with the lamp and my chair until the boys called the police out of sheer terror.

Troy left for a few days, and while he was away, I had planned to give him the master bedroom and move out my home office. But I had broken my arm in a cycling accident and couldn't do any lifting. So instead, I cleaned out the spare room, closets and all, and made a nice space for him when he returned. When I told him that I would be taking the master bedroom since I couldn't move my furniture, he became belligerent. "This is my room, my bed, my house! You can get the fuck out! This is where I masturbate!" I proceeded to stay at my desk as I was still working, and he took his clothes off and started jerking off, all the while verbally abusing me and mocking me for being too damaged to "fuck" him. The fact that he was getting sexual gratification from his own rage while cruelly berating me was clearly an indicator that I was not safe and I needed to ask him to move out, despite our original agreement to share the house until the divorce was finalized.

If narcissists have a handbook, he followed it to the letter to punish me and get the upper hand: blame, aggression, intimidation, verbal abuse, mockery, deception, and sabotage. Once I was deemed his enemy, he attacked with a vengeance. His biggest revenge was when he refused to go back to North Dakota and run the businesses that held our 1.5 million of community assets. He said he would just run the businesses to the ground since I obviously didn't want him to work there. As a result, he cheated me out of my share of $750,000 when all was said and done, claiming his businesses were in ruins, thanks to me. And as a result, he didn't have to pay a dime of alimony. My attorney had never met anyone quite like him and said repeatedly that she didn't know how I had stayed with him for so long. Even the mediator, a retired judge, described Troy as clearly unstable and living in an alternate reality. He considered him dangerous and warned me to get the locks changed in the house once he moved out.

During one of the earlier altercations, a day or so after I had dropped the deadly D- bomb, I said to Troy, "Oh my God! You are being such an asshole. Just stop!"

He responded, with dripping sarcasm, "Oh my God! Oh my God! I don't know why you are saying that. You don't even have a god. Do you? Well, do you?" I don't know how to add the bitter, hateful tenor to the words in order to adequately replicate the mood, but his suppressed rage was finally being exposed regarding my de-conversion.

I responded, "What's even more interesting is that you *do* have a God, and yet you are still acting this way. Your actions certainly aren't very Christian."

"Oh, you don't know a damned thing about Christianity!"

"Really? Fifty years as a believer and I know nothing? How about you, Troy, are you a Christian?"

At the top of his lungs and with the angry force of a freight train, his words reverberated off my ears and off the walls. *"No, I'm not!"*

I most certainly didn't see that coming. I didn't know if he just didn't "feel" like a Christian in that moment or if the divorce had become the straw that broke the camel's back and he truly was done with Christianity. Regardless, the hypocrisy did not go unnoticed. His pharisaical disgust with me for not drinking the Kool-Aid was like Ted Haggart publicly preaching against drugs and homosexuality while doing meth and banging male prostitutes. This was a case of the pot calling the kettle black. So much of the sting over the years was Troy's claim to be such a great spiritual giant, family man, mentor, and marriage counselor, when behind the scenes he was often a mean schoolyard bully. A few days later, I went into his office and noticed all his theology books were missing from his shelves. Had he sold them, tossed them, or just boxed them up and put them in storage? I had no idea. I wondered if he really had renounced his faith. If so, he was keeping this secret to himself because he continued to attend Bible study and church, just as he had done for the last thirty years. The sympathy he was getting from the Christian community was likely what he needed in order to play the poor helpless victim, being blindsided with the divorce and kicked out of his own house for "no reason."

After ten long brutal months and several failed mediations, we finally settled. There is no way to divorce a narcissist and come out a winner, and I finally cut my losses and settled against my attorney's counsel. She strongly objected and even refused to sign the papers because it was so unfair, but I didn't care. I just wanted to be done with the divorce and done with him. I needed closure.

The day the papers were signed, I was heading back to my car and my stomach started immediately cramping up as I was stricken with diarrhea. (TMI? Sorry!) It felt as though my body was finally ready to let go of all the toxic stress I had been subconsciously holding on to and I was on the road to healing and wholeness.

"This was supposed to be *'til death do us part,*" I pondered sadly, on the way home, letting the reality sink in that I was officially divorced. But then I had an epiphany. The wife that Troy had married thirty-one years ago no longer existed. She was a believer whose ideas, opinions, desires, thoughts, and emotions had been dictated and imposed on her by the Bible and by her faith. He loved the submissive, God-fearing, church-going, Sunday school–teaching, Republican Christian wife. But that person was no more. She died when her faith imploded, obliterating her very existence. So I could in fact say that I had kept my vow "'til death do us part."

"This is what happens when you take your eyes off the Lord," cautioned one Christian friend to another in her self-righteous, gossipy tone, guised as a prayer request. Ironically though, it wasn't that I had taken my eyes off Jesus; it's that I started looking more closely! It was only when I confronted my cognitive dissonance that my faith started to collapse. And my marriage followed suit because it had been built on the same faulty foundation. The physical, emotional, and verbal abuse left indelible scars that were never adequately addressed, and my departure from faith merely exposed the damage and helped me see the hidden layers buried beneath the happy façade of faith.

The courage it took to admit that my religion and my marriage no longer worked for me and to let them go is nothing less than astounding, considering the ramifications. I trust that the same fortitude and inner grit will continue to guide me as I seek to honor the new "me" who has come up for air.

It may take a while to unravel the effects of early childhood abuse and neglect, terrifying religious indoctrination, and domestic violence. I believe the next chapters of my story will be the best ones yet.

Recently, without the help of the Holy Spirit, serenading cherubim, or rhyming harbingers, I found the love of my life—a smart, gentle, funny, romantic free spirit, a liberal, like-minded atheist whom I adore.

And if you've made it this far in my story, you deserve to be let in on one final revelation—another layer of "me" exposed when all vestiges of my old thought patterns were stripped away:

My sweetheart's name is Jeanene.

About the Author

Joy Hopper currently teaches elementary school in the Pacific Northwest by day, runs an Airbnb from her basement by night, and attempts to whittle away at her bucket list on weekends and summers. Despite having stepped foot on all seven continents, taught abroad, cycled across the country, composed children's musicals, earned her master's at age fifty, and published her memoir, she has no intention of slowing down any time soon.

The people in her world who make her both insane and insanely happy are her six amazing kids, who continue to be the object of her unconditional love and pure delight. She claims, when she grows up, she wants to be just like them.

CPSIA information can be obtained
at www.ICGtesting.com
Printed in the USA
LVOW03s1910250318
571086LV00001B/39/P